OPS IN A WIMPY

Memoirs of a sub-hunting pilot

Graham Harrison

First published in Great Britain 2017

Copyright © 2017 by Graham Harrison

The moral right of the author has been asserted.

No part of this book may be used or reproduced in any manner whatsoever without written permission from the publisher except in the case of brief quotations embodied in critical articles or reviews.

Every reasonable effort has been made to trace copyright holders of material reproduced in this book, but if any have been inadvertently overlooked the publishers would be glad to hear from them.

Also by Graham Harrison
(under the name H Grayson):

The Last Alderman

Non Stop Review

Cover illustration: Tom's Wellington

For the Harrison family

The author, Venice, 2015

Ops in a Wimpy, Ops in a Wimpy
Who'll come on ops in a Wimpy with me?
And they sang in the flames
As they pranged upon the hangar roof
Who'll come on ops in a Wimpy with me?

(Chorus, sung to the tune of *Waltzing Matilda*)

* * *

The absence of a front gun turret in the maritime marque of the Wellington made the aircraft's nose section into a sort of retreat or bower . . .

"*On a clear night the dark sheen of the sea – surprisingly close and, in retrospect, often with a wavy moonpath – would be visible through the rounded perspex nose, which even when blind with rain seemed protective of the bower.*

Since almost all our patrols took us over Biscay I thought of this transparency as my Bay Window, a reminder of the one in the front bedroom at home for which mother Nellie had commenced crocheting net curtains with a pattern of stags and trees during the air raids of 1940-41. This homely connection further enhanced the nose section's secret charm."

Glossary

EFTS	Elementary Flying Training School
F/O	Flying Officer
NCO	Non-Commissioned Officer
OTU	Operational Training Unit
P/O	Pilot Officer
Wop/Ag	Wireless Operator/Air Gunner
U/T	Under Training

Contents

Foreword	1
The Reason Why	3
Into the Blue	11
Between Wars	48
A Sea Change	88
Cook's Tour	153
Alf Revisited	167
High Wood	169
Afterword	175

FOREWORD

The author's experience as a Coastal Command Wellington pilot flying anti-U-boat patrols over the Bay of Biscay and North-West approaches between 1943 and 1945 forms the core of these memoirs.

Having been led to expect a fighter role following training in Canada, he was not best pleased to find himself flying for up to ten hours, in all sorts of weather, over a darkened sea, searching for U-boats which obstinately remained *Untersee* to avoid the aircraft's radar.

But gradually, the close bond between crew members which was a feature of long-distance operational flying, and the humour which relieved tensions during flight, worked their magic, and on a moonlit night between spells at the controls there was even time to indulge in dreams of sexual conquest unrealised in the straight-laced thirties.

Catching a U-boat on the surface in the seas surrounding Britain became an increasingly rare event once the Kriegsmarine had given its U-boats the means of detecting aircraft radar transmissions, giving them time to submerge. The author's first encounter with a so-called iron coffin came at the war's end when a surprisingly large number popped up to surrender.

Until then, day and night patrols had given them no respite, forcing them to proceed submerged at greatly reduced speed, with morale-destroying consequences. This, with the diversion of more four-engined 'heavies' from Bomber to Coastal Command led to victory in the Battle of the Atlantic, allowing the vital convoys to proceed virtually unhindered.

After the war's end the author abandoned his Wimpy for the more comfortable DC3 Dakota, spending his remaining six months as an airman flying diplomats and other VIPs to exotic destinations in the Far East. The high spot was a trip from Burma to Hong Kong with a company of ENSA, headed by John Gielgud, who were performing Hamlet and Blithe Spirit to demob-happy troops awaiting repatriation.

Life on the home front revolves round mother Nellie after the disappearance of WW1-wounded father Alfred. As well as rescuing the family business, she successfully brings up their three children, never re-marrying. After her death the author traces his father and they meet amicably. Some years later a half-brother gets in touch, they become friends, and the memoir ends with a Great War battlefields tour – when both stand in silence near the shattered wood on the Somme where their father had been gravely wounded

THE REASON WHY

In November 2007 my almost-forgotten wartime pilot's log book sprang to life.

I'd picked up the current issue of *Flypast* from the row-on-row of magazines in a local newsagents, attracted by the cover illustration of a Gloster Gladiator, to my mind the handsomest of the last crop of biplane fighters. Flicking through for a free look (I hadn't bought a flying magazine since, as we used to say, Pontius was a pilot) I was tickled to find an illustrated article on 612 Squadron, a U-boat-hunting outfit of Coastal Command. This was one of a series about RAF auxiliary units formed in the run-up to the second world war and 'adopted' by local communities, in this case the county of Aberdeen.

Wellington Mk IV: 612 Squadron

There, flying off the page, was a 612 Wellington, recognisably one I'd actually flown in as second pilot between October 1943 and July

1944 before leaving for an Operational Training Unit (OTU) and subsequently joining another squadron as aircraft captain.

Its attempt to disguise itself as a Hawker Typhoon by sprouting under-wing rocket launchers hadn't come off – they must have been added soon after I'd left when the squadron moved from Devon to the east coast where it saw out the war in an anti-shipping role.

Of course I had to fork out for the magazine, but not wishing to be taken for an ageing WW2 freak I mentioned the coincidence in tendering my £3.80, receiving an 'Oh, yes?' look from the young assistant.

The author of the piece, heroically-named Murdo McMorton, had included information on the squadron, much of which was new to me – or forgotten. In an appreciative letter to the editor I pointed out my connection with 612 and this appeared in the January 2008 issue.

Shortly afterwards, the editor forwarded a letter from a Nottingham reader who wrote that his uncle, a Wireless Operator/Air Gunner (Wop/Ag) on the squadron, was lost with his crew in the early hours of 30 October 1943 off Cape Ortegal in the Bay of Biscay during an attack on U-415. The pilot had carried out a strafing run before dropping four depth charges. These had done enough damage to send the submarine back to Brest – after its 20mm gun had scored hits on the aircraft, which crashed burning into the sea killing the crew of six.

Had Mr Harrison any recollection of his uncle or the rest of the crew?

The answer was 'No'. We had just joined the squadron and hadn't yet got to know other crews, but it looked from the log book entry covering our second operation as if his uncle's aircraft and ours had been in roughly the same area of the Bay on the night of 29/30 October:

```
Anti-shipping reco:
        Isle de Bas to Ushant* A/S patrol 6.35 hours (Night)
```

If he could send further information . . .

---

* *Anglicised version of Isle de Batz and Oussantse*

RAF Coastal Command, 1939-45: Ops Room at Eastbury Park, Northwood

He did, including a map of the area from which it was clear that their 'box patrol' had started where ours terminated, ending near the Spanish coast where U-boats passing between their French coastal bases and the Atlantic killing grounds were known to skulk under the protection of Spanish territorial waters. We would have been briefed together and the large chart on the ops-room wall would have featured a U-boat symbol in the search area.

It was their luck to find it, ours to return to a breakfast of bacon and eggs. I had no recollection of the incident, which wasn't surprising as minimal drama attended the failure of an aircraft to return from patrol.

The correspondent was grateful for the information and thanked me on behalf of his mother and aunt, the uncle's sisters (the grief never goes away).

The editor then sent me another response, this time from someone researching aspects of the Verdon-Roe family, founders of the Avro company which produced the Lancaster bomber, and later the Shackleton reconnaissance aircraft. Had I, asked the researcher, come across Anthony Verdon, scion of the family and pilot on the squadron whose aircraft disappeared over the Bay on March 17 1944 after failing to respond to a bad weather recall signal? Two other aircraft out that night had returned safely.

I replied that whilst I had no recollection of Verdon or his crew there was the following entry in my log book for 16 March 1944:

```
A/S Patrol: recalled weather: 5.45hrs: night
```

– confirmation that we were indeed one of the two aircraft that returned safely. Sadly, Anthony had married two weeks before his final flight. The last verse of *Wellington Pilot*, a poem by Pamela Gillilan,* a wartime WAAF, says it all:

> *A college boy, fair-haired*
> *Prankish to hold off fate.*
> *I'd watched the ops board*
> *For his name.*
> *A night erased him –*
> *Sweep of the duster,*
> *Soft fall of chalk.*

There was a third response of a less doleful kind from a collector of RAF log books (!) who had come across a Flying Officer Harrison as

---

* *The All-Steel Traveller: Bloodaxe Books 1994*

pilot of a DC3 Dakota in which the log book's original owner had crewed as navigator on a Rangoon-Delhi round trip in April 1946. Was I he? The affirmative answer took me back over sixty years to the post-war Cook's Tour of the far east at His Majesty's expense, the high spot of which was transporting a company of ENSA (the forces entertainment outfit), headed by John Gielgud, performing *Hamlet* and *Blithe Spirit* in rotation between Burma and Hong Kong.

* * *

About a year after the *Flypast* revelations the mystery surrounding another loss of aircraft and crew was solved, this one of personal and family interest.

Denis, a fellow pupil at grammar school though two years my senior, lived near us in the Leicester suburb to which we'd decamped in 1929 from a terrace in the city. Though not a close friend he became a regular visitor after father Alf's disappearance following the move, enjoying the informality of our father-free ménage and mother Nellie's liberated sense of fun.

He became very fond of my younger sister who at the time was living with our two maiden aunts in their Leicester boarding house, returning home most weekends. Mildred recalls:

He often took me back to the aunts on Sunday evening and was so kind to me in a brotherly way, taking me to the cinema, swimming and so on. About a year before the outbreak of war he asked mum if he could take me to Portsmouth – by then in the RAF he had a pass permitting him to go round all the aircraft carriers and see everything on offer. Mum agreed and made me a white blazer with my initials embroidered on the pocket. He said how proud he was to take me which made me feel a million dollars! One memory – being a chocoholic – is of the enormous Easter eggs he used to bring to aunties' for me. They were always in a box, covered with sugar flowers – almost too good to eat, though of course I did!

Denis had left school at sixteen to work in Leicester's leading grocery chain, which traded under the banner *Let Worthingtons Feed You*. After a year or so he got fed up with the routine and in 1937 joined the RAF as a wireless operator, later adding air gunnery to his skills. In April 1940 he was reported missing, believed killed, on a bombing operation, leaving family and friends with that special grief engendered by disappearance, as it were, into thin air.

Nothing more was heard of him until, towards the end of 2008, Mildred was astonished to see his photograph in uniform above a *Leicester Mercury* news item about the discovery of the buried remains of the Hampden bomber in which he'd flown on his last operation. A team from the Air Crash Investigation and Archaeology Group had identified the site in a farm field near to St Mary's Lighthouse in Whitley Bay, Northumberland, and with information from the Air Historical Branch of the Ministry of Defence the story of the bomber's last flight could now be told.

It was a tragic tale. The aircraft was one of six from 83 Squadron based at Scampton in Lincolnshire detailed to bomb shipping off Sylt on the night of 6/7 April 1940.

There was evidence that it had returned damaged without having dropped its bombs, making a landfall at Whitley Bay where, after circling the lighthouse signalling SOS, three of the crew baled out over the sea, drowning before they could be recovered. Identified remains proved that Denis had still been on board – probably wounded or dead – and was destroyed by the exploding bombs. Searchlight beams directed towards a nearby airfield had not been followed, probably because an emergency landing with full bombload might have destroyed the aircraft and endangered those on the ground.

Mildred got in touch with one of Denis's never-seen nieces mentioned in the *Mercury* article who told her that in two days' time a memorial service was to be held at the no-longer-operational lighthouse. She couldn't go: could I? I could, though to arrive in time for the afternoon service would mean a dawn start with wife Sue doing most of the driving. Truth to tell I rather relished the trip as during the sixties I'd lived in Whitley Bay for about four years with my late wife and our family and had rarely been back. I still missed the Geordie humour ('It was at Whitley Bay that me old uncle Hal had failed to teach us to swim' – Alex Glasgow) and if ambition hadn't vaulted me back to the Midlands I'd have been happy to remain.

We were both glad to have made the effort. An RAF helicopter dipped in salute as we followed an Air Training Corps group along the causeway which at low tide led to the lighthouse, to be met by Denis's 93 year-old sister and her three daughters, supported by a Group Captain from the airfield the aircraft had never reached, the local vicar, RAF ex-servicemen, members of the Archaeological Group and of the Friends of St Mary's Island.

Denis Sharpe at a training camp

A plaque was unveiled bearing the names of the crew, and among the memorabilia displayed were letters Denis had written home shortly before his disappearance with photographs of him and the aircraft. The navigator was named as Pilot Officer (P/O) Keith Brooke-Taylor, and surmising that he must have been related to the

Brooke-Taylor of radio and TV fame I later wrote to him at the BBC but received no reply.

I still find it astonishing that poor Denis should have risen as it were from the dead in this way. *More astonishingly, the crash site was within half a mile of our 1960's house from which I must many times have walked Oscar, our spaniel, over Denis's buried remains.*

* * *

A la recherche du temps perdu! Having recently struggled through a marathon read of a new translation of Proust's epic it occurred to me that if the author recently described as 'the sensitive asthmatic insomniac who can't recall anything until he dips a Madeleine into a cup of tea' could *recherche* six volumes-worth while cooped up in a sound-proofed room surely, between walking the dog and mowing the lawns, I could manage just one in my cluttered study? I unearthed the fragments of a long-abandoned autobiography, advised wife Sue to practise being a widow and started Prousting. And, as we say in the West Country – *'ere 'tis.*

INTO THE BLUE

J. Wellington Wimpy

First, a word about the Wellington, which is likely to impress its unique character on the chapters that follow. For those so dazzled by the film star glamour of the Spitfire, Hurricane, Mosquito and Lancaster that the history and sterling qualities of this much-loved aircraft may have escaped them, and bearing in mind that, uniquely, it served in its original role throughout the war, I offer the following profile in the digestible form suggested by the question-and-answer *Ithaca* chapter of James Joyce's *Ulysses*, A Wimpthaca:

A trip round the aircraft

Who designed it?	Barnes Wallis, later knighted, who went on to invent obscenely huge bombs.
What was the distinguishing feature of the design?	The aircraft's geodetic or basket-weave construction.
Why was it so named?	Its predecessor was the Wellesley – family name of the hero of Waterloo. When the single-engine aircraft was redesigned as a twin it was the happy thought to reflect in its name Sir Arthur's ennoblement.
Would this have gratified His Grace?	Initially, yes, but his pride would undoubtedly have been dented by its early nickname, Wimpy – after J. Wellington Wimpy the hamburger-eating character in the Popeye cartoons.

Was its nickname the only reason for its perceived lack of gravitas?	Sadly, no. When standing it undoubtedly had a droopy-drawers appearance. Also, those who confessed to flying in Wellingtons were the butt of such rejoinders as, 'Good God! Don't they issue you with flying boots?'
Was this fair?	Not entirely. Airborne, in white maritime livery with undercarriage retracted, the tall tailfin and wide wingspan lent it a certain grace which, with the distinctive whistle of its Bristol engines suggested, if not a swan, perhaps a snow goose. Its gently undulating wings heightened this impression.
Undulating wings? Alarming, surely?	Some, flying in it for the first time, were given to remark, 'Jesus, the kite flies by flapping its wings!' But the phenomenon was due to the geodetics. Vickers chief test pilot, 'Mutt' Summers, once joked, 'If you looped it the wings touched.'
Looped it? Not in a bomber!	Ken Wallis, a Wimpy veteran, was said to be quite happy to perform aerobatics during fighter affiliation exercises but was told to 'tone it down'.
Where was the aircraft's main point of entry and exit?	On the underside of the nose, by means of a ladder, stowed on the starboard side of the cockpit.

Did this arrangement invite comment?	It did. Groundcrew were known to break into the George Formby song *When I'm cleaning windows*, with fantasy ukulele accompaniment when aircrew ascended the ladder. Before they wore battledress trousers, WAAFs engaged on maintenance work within the fuselage often complained that male groundstaff would linger at the foot of the ladder as they ascended or descended.
Was the Wellington consigned to honourable retirement after its role as long-range bomber was taken over by Stirlings, Halifaxes and Lancasters?	No, it remained operational throughout the conflict – notably in Coastal Command and as a medium range bomber in the Middle East. One of its more bizarre roles was exploding magnetic mines (for which it was fitted with a large-diameter degaussing apparatus, when it was known as 'The Flying Ring').
What were its principal roles in Coastal Command?	General reconnaissance; anti-shipping strikes in the Mediterranean; anti-U-boat patrols, mainly in the Bay of Biscay, when it was fitted with a retractable searchlight known as a Leigh Light.
After what or whom was the searchlight so named?	Its inventor, Squadron Leader Humphrey de Verde Leigh, pictured in illustrations as a rather dour officer, chest adorned with drooping wings above a row of faded medal ribbons known as fruit salad.

Was the light effective against U-boats?	Initially, yes, especially in the Bay of Biscay where they were accustomed to surface at night to recharge the batteries used for underwater propulsion, in transit to or from their pens on the French coast. After the fitting of improved aircraft radar they took counter-measures such as staying submerged at night and fighting it out in daytime with improved armament.
What was the likely reaction of crew members of a surfaced U-boat when on its first deployment they were illuminated by the light?	To those on deck enjoying a breath of Biscay air and an ersatz cigar, a midnight sun swooping towards them at sea level spitting tracer and defecating depth charges is said to have done wonders for the constipation from which many *Unterseebooters* suffered through poor diet and lack of exercise.
Who operated the light?	The retractable turret amidships containing the light would be lowered and raised hydraulically by one of the three Wop/Ags while the second dicky, flat out on the bench, would direct it onto the target by operating a sort of joystick. At the same time another crew member standing astride him would be firing the free-standing Brownings through the vengeful nose of the aerial Moby Dick.

Is there truth in the legend that in 1940 a lone Wellington breached Swiss neutrality to drop a parachute bomb in the vicinity of the Zurich house in which the author James Joyce was living?

There is no trace in squadron records or the Public Record Office of such a flight. The rumour is thought to have originated with an irate Fenian from County Cork who, incensed by the 'blasphemous smut' in the novel *Ulysses* (which he had not read), was heard to say: 'They should drop a bomb on the dirty-minded atheist!'

Some who flew long night patrols in the aircraft were said to endow it with aphrodisiac properties. Was this true?

Read on . . .

A Wellington instrument panel

Tumescence in the Clouds

The absence of a front gun turret in the maritime marque of the Wellington made the aircraft's nose section into a sort of retreat or bower. This was enhanced by a long bench covering the accumulators which powered the Leigh Light.

The bench was covered in leather – or perhaps rexine – or then again it might have been the genuine article. All those craftsmen and women in the factories at Weybridge, Chester and Blackpool lovingly assembling Barnes Wallis's intricate geodetic framework probably had to be restrained from smocking the fuselage fabric and finishing off the pilot's seat cushion in *broderie anglaise.*

Before call-up I had just managed to reach the seventh pillar of T.E. Lawrence's *magnum opus* and so it flattered my literary pretensions (and added to the bench's allure) that in length and smoothness it fitted the description of the one in his Cloud's Hill cottage I'd read about not long after his fatal accident in 1936 on *Boanerges*, the Brough Superior motorcycle.

It was heavenly after my stint at the controls to stoop down into the nose and stretch out on the bench after pouring coffee from the crew-size flask. On a clear night the dark sheen of the sea – surprisingly close and, in retrospect, often with a wavy moonpath – would be visible through the rounded perspex nose, which even when blind with rain seemed protective of the bower. Since almost all our patrols took us over Biscay I thought of this transparency as my Bay Window, a reminder of the one in the front bedroom at home for which mother Nellie had commenced crocheting net curtains with a pattern of stags and trees during the air raids of 1940-41. This homely connection further enhanced the nose section's secret charm.

The duties of a Coastal Command second pilot were not onerous, as the pejorative 'second dicky' suggests, and it had quickly become clear after crewing-up that our Flight Lieutenant captain was not of the press-on-regardless school of pilots whose lust for distinction in action could turn a routine patrol into a series of dangerous attempts to seek out and engage the enemy at all costs. This was understandable as he had already completed a tour on Bristol Beaufort bombers and spent his 'rest' towing drogues for Under Training (U/T) air gunners to shoot at ('Far more dangerous than ops!').

So, during the steady running of the hours on a long patrol, there was ample time between spells at the controls, pumping fuel from auxiliary to main tanks, keeping the engines log and provisioning the crew to indulge my fantasies, which, as with most single males just into their twenties, were mostly about sex. In the vibrating darkness would be erected shimmering castles of voluptuousness in whose every silken chamber complaisant women yielded up their treasures in a rich variety of attitudes: spread-eagled on the bench swathed in dishevelled shrouds of a released parachute ('Keep your knees off the bomb panel, my love.'); midships with candle-white arms braced against the main wing spar ('My lord did me the honour twice, standing in his flying boots.'); and even a lap-top interlude in the cramped but romantically moonlit rear gun turret ('The Browning version!').

Sometimes our patrols would take us close to the Spanish coast and I remember seeing on several occasions the lights of Coruna shining in the dark landmass, disappearing as we wheeled back into the Bay towards the stygian Kingdom. From then on my dreams, sleeping and waking, were of escape from the battered grey aircraft carrier which Britain had become to somewhere shining with warmth, light and love.

I was aware that Stanley (one of the three Wop/Ags) who cruelly missed his newly married wife – especially as the periodical two-weeks aircrew leave approached – also indulged in similar flights of sexual fancy during his two-hour spells in the rear turret before taking his turn at wireless and radar. He would have the glimmering crown of light in view for some time before night and distance swallowed it, and the spell it cast over him would last for days. 'All those Spanish bints dancing fit to drop, skirts round their ears, showing all they've got. Jesus, if we'd have been nearer I'd have baled out and got among them!' On our return out would come the much-thumbed photograph, circulating at the time, of Carmen Miranda dancing the fandango with Cesar Romero, purporting to show that underneath the swirling frills was only the essential Carmen – though careful study never convinced me.

During these airborne dream-times my limited real-life experiences would be passed in review, each forming a bead in the meagre rosary of girls who had allowed my fumbling fingers to explore their hidden landscapes, commencing with the schoolgirl up whose navy knickers my hand had been thrust by a friend bent on raising me to the same platform of experience as himself.

None of the beads marked the achievement of what Somerset Maugham had coldly called 'sexual congress', although this was nothing unusual in the thirties when in all but the highest and lowest ranks of society religion, respectability, parental vigilance and the dubious safety and lust-suppressing effects of birth control methods all conspired to keep people's parts apart until marriage or at least 'engagement'. When the teenage, hair-platted only child of near neighbours became pregnant by her carefully groomed boyfriend the parents found it necessary to move away.

Even in Canada, that land of sexual opportunity for U/T pilots and navigators on the Commonwealth Air Training Scheme, the tousle-haired aviator eternally grinning from within the buffalo-hide covers of the photograph album had failed to get beyond first base with the pictured high school girl who would wave as his Tiger Moth all but brushed her bedroom window on a Manitoba morning.

The Elementary Flying Training School (EFTS) was near the small town of Neepawa – a Cree word meaning 'Land of Plenty'. Its citizens were so welcoming that we took more seriously than usual the pre-embarkation pep talk: *'Each of you is an ambassador for your country. You will behave accordingly!'* Obediently, I played the nice English boy so convincingly that the girl's father practically promised me the succession to his hardware store should I return after the war, whilst Mom had intuited that I was not the sort to venture beyond the rolled stocking-tops which rendered Canadian girls so much more vulnerable than their suspender-belted English opposite numbers, some of whose underwear one almost expected to be mouse-trapped. I even won over crusty Gran by defying a confinement to camp and presenting her with a bag of candies.

Author and friends at Neepawa in a Tiger Moth DH82

Neepawa, Manitoba, from the air

Having satisfied both the flying and written tests I moved westward to a Service Flying Training School (SFTS) near the town of Moosejaw, Saskatchewan, appropriately situated near a bend in the Moose River.

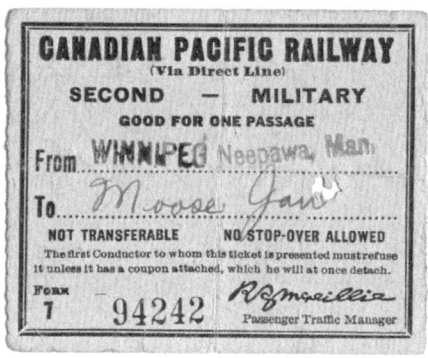

CPR ticket, Neepawa to Moosejaw

This was – and I believe still is – Canada's primary military flying training centre, and it was here that I fell head-over-tailfin in love with the North American Harvard II, a single-engine advanced trainer for would-be fighter pilots in which I rolled, looped and flew low enough to terrify the prairie cattle as well as the flight commander on my passing-out test.

Harvards in vic formation, Moosejaw

'Overconfident' is the comment in my log book and I have often wondered whether the wingless wonder at the Air Ministry who later assigned me to Coastal Command did so with some such comment as: 'That'll calm the bugger down and save a Spitfire!'

Author in a Harvard

Harvard instrument panel – note the fighter controls

I was 'winged' at an airfield further west in the province of Alberta, rejoicing in the name of Medicine Hat, where the coveted flying badge was pinned to my chest by Billy Bishop, a much-decorated Canadian airman of the first world war.

The affair with the Harvard having left little or no room for girls, I enjoyed an unexpected sexual *frisson* during a final fling at the Calgary Stampede – the annual celebration of life on the prairies, where, in addition to the rodeo-ing, hot dogging and banana splitting, I had my first taste of striptease.

In fact, the stripping had already taken place when I entered the marquee. The tease was the crossed hands of the naked girl, immobile on a plinth, covering the spot which in classical paintings was often screened by a fig leaf (I later learned that Maupassant had named his rowing boat on the Seine '*la renverse de la feuille*', which translated as 'the other side of the leaf').

The elderly woman introducing the girl did so with a remark which I have never forgotten: '*I used to pose like this but now my hands are not big enough.*'

The failure to break my sexual duck in Canada doesn't in retrospect stand out as all that tragic. For one thing, a studio portrait of the girl who later became my wife arrived at this time to stimulate home thoughts from abroad. For another, it was Canada itself I'd fallen in love with. Although after the long months of training I was looking forward to rejoining the war as an operational pilot, it was sad to be leaving the warm hospitality and limitless landscapes – so liberating after the Kingdom's constricting patchwork. I felt regret – guilt almost – at abandoning the many good people I'd met to the long winter nights, their isolation emphasised by the haunting moan of the locomotives hauling their long trains across the frozen prairies.

As the stripped-down Queen Elizabeth liner pulled out of Halifax harbour for its six-day unescorted sprint across the Atlantic, Bing Crosby's *White Christmas* fog-horned us on our way. *En route* I supposed that most of the sardined pilots, navigators, returning instructors and groundstaff were like me facing with such courage as could be mustered the prospect of swapping the T-bone steaks, ice cream and banana splits played down in letters home for the rationed hard tack the answering airmail letters tried not to complain about.

Most, I supposed, would be looking forward to their first pint of warm beer in a pub free of the disturbing sight of Canadian drinkers shaking salt into the chill beer-parlor offering to make it drinkable, a habit partly excused by their salty sense of humour (I still have somewhere the printed card handed to me by the editor of the Neepawa Press, Manitoba – 'Doers of good things in print on paper': *Come to our grand donkey barbecue. Everybody gets a piece of ass!*)

My own fantasies, jammed up against the cabin ceiling, centred on the triumphs which long absence and the contents of my kitbag would surely facilitate. Fluffy fur mittens, silk stockings, Klondyke-gold trinkets, boxes of candy . . . I visualised the licked lips and lack-luxury expressions of my small circle of girl friends as I poured these treasures before them like a Zanzibar trader bartering for slaves.

Of course this did not happen. Mother Nellie and my two maiden aunts nudged me towards worthier recipients for largesse and the prize gifts ended up in the Christmas stockings of sisters Peggy and Mildred, and the girl marked down as my fate. Consolation prizes, none of a quality to tip favours beyond the sticking point, were shared between an outer circle including several girls who had joined the services or were doing war work – one, of fairly easy morals, turning up for a cinema date in Land Army *breeches* which I didn't attempt to penetrate, contenting myself with the bovine breastworks.

I remember feeling at the time a mixture of irritation at having allowed my better nature to be exploited in this way and the overall feeling that this was the right thing to do anyway. It was also the point at which I came to terms with my lack of the predatory sexual instinct, noted and half-admired in a couple of ex-public school U/T pilots who would return from forays in Winnipeg or Regina to entertain us after lights out with accounts of ruthless sexual encounters of which the Marquis de Sade might not have been ashamed.

This genuine killer instinct would have been recognised by the thick-ringed lords of the Air Ministry, and no doubt both sexual sadists became ace fighter pilots with more decorations than Nellie and Mildred were hanging on the artificial Christmas tree as I burst into the living room of our home, *Greyfell.*

Why Fly?

I wish I could say with Yeats that it was —

> *A lonely impulse of delight*
> *Drove to this tumult in the clouds* *

but I can't. What drove was a summons to present myself at a Leicester recruitment centre. Neither I nor any close friend had rushed to the colours on the outbreak of war as had father Alf and thousands more in 1914 (as if, in Larkin's words, '*it were all an August Bank Holiday lark.*' †) Only 'Gats', a member of our informal cycling club whose speciality was collecting and firing antique pistols, had volunteered, and he was among the hundreds of sailors lost when *HMS Royal Oak* was torpedoed at anchorage in Scapa Flow soon after war was declared.

I was content on my eighteenth birthday in March 1939 to register for national service and await call-up, myself and others of a predominantly left-wing persuasion having briefly flirted with conscientious objection before deciding that it would take more courage than we possessed. During the Great War Grandpa Harrison, who lived in comparative luxury about three miles from us, had joined in the campaign against a local conchie who ran a popular 'boathouse club' on the sluggish Soar — which some of us frequented and whose business never really recovered.

Himself a prosperous tailor and outfitter, Tom Harrison had served his country by selling mourning garments in great numbers to relatives of 'the fallen', since in those days even the poorest strove to observe the full funereal formalities. Fond as I was of him, I instinctively sided with anyone who felt inclined to resist a rerun of the 1914-18

---

* *An Irish Airman Foresees His Death. Collected poems: MacMillan & Co 1933*
† *MCMXIV: The Whitsun Weddings: Faber and Faber 1988*

shambles. It was only a few years since the Daily Express, in full cry with its anti-war campaign, had published a pictorial history of the war containing photographs of startling candour. The propped-up corpse of a German soldier, decayed features under coal-scuttle helmet, skeleton hands raised as if warding off a bayonet lunge, was a shock example of the anti-war mood. Its caption, so far as I recall it, echoed Wilfred Owen's *pity of war*:

    Ich hat ein Vaterland. Es war ein traum.

So it was no surprise that I was singularly unmilitant. The final straw had been the failure of the government to support Spain's republican regime in the civil war against Franco which, as refugees arrived in Leicester, did inspire me and a few other hotheads to attend a 'Volunteers for Spain' meeting at the Secular Hall in the city centre – which received short shrift when reported to Nellie.

  Certainly I had no interest in flying apart from having read a small part of the Biggles *oeuvre* and a few potted biographies of Great War aces before discovering more fertile literary fields. The only live airman I'd encountered was Mr Warren, a professional pilot who lived nearby with his tribe of cheeky children, and who regularly buzzed overhead in a small biplane. He was a large, red-faced man, more son of the soil than inspirational knight of the air.

  The airship R101 which glided wraith-like over Leicester in 1930 seemed more of a menace to a nine-year-old than an invitation to join the triumph of the skies. Indeed, following its crash in France shortly afterwards with the loss of all hands including the Air Minister, a terrified ten-year-old Leicester lad who'd fired his air rifle at the dirigible as it passed overhead went to ground for some days in the belief that it was he who had been the cause of its delayed demise.[*]

  As the phoney war (to which Dunkirk and the Blitz soon put paid) wore on into the spring of 1940 with no word about call-up it began to seem possible that Hitler and Mussolini might yet turn out to be more akin to their *doppelgängers* Charlie Chaplin and Jack Oakie than

---

[*] *The Boy Who Shot Down an Airship:* Michael Green (Heinemann)

to the ogres depicted in the war cartoons. Mussolini had anyway never shed his musical comedy air – 'Abyssinia' could still be heard on errand boys' lips as a jokey 'see you' long after his cowardly campaign had disappeared from the headlines. Dispatches from the Maginot Line in the foreign language magazine I was taking (*'Rien a signaller!'*) had induced the half-hope that the worst might not happen – at least to us.

I felt – and still feel – more than a twinge of sympathy for Chamberlain in his efforts to avoid all-out war, though during the final efforts to propitiate the Führer I'd joined in the general snigger at his French nickname – *M. J'aime Berlin*. Those who condemn him tend to forget how unthinkable the prospect of a re-run of the Great War was to a generation which had lived in its shadow.

On the declaration of war, press pictures had shown Chamberlain in formal black, top hat dead level above harrowed countenance, shoes (boots perhaps?) brightly polished – reminder of a press photograph taken in happier times over the caption: *Mr Chamberlain is always well turned out.*

When he *was* turned out I recollect little enthusiasm for Churchill. The instant confidence which the nation is supposed to have felt on his accession was not my experience or that of my friends as for years he'd been regarded as a party-switching rogue politician, mainly responsible for the Gallipoli disaster. Ronald, one of my two close friends, then at university, captured the feeling in a letter:

> *Churchill? Bitter pill! What's to do? Hullabaloo!*

Almost a year after registration I was called to the recruitment centre for medical examination and – depending on the result – choice of service. During that unreal period I immersed myself in all things Arabic after reading Lawrence's *Seven Pillars of Wisdom*, an eighteenth birthday present, and Burton's *Arabia Deserta*. Having also become aware of Compton Mackenzie's adventures as a wartime spy in those parts I conceived the idea of volunteering for the secret service and disappearing into the Middle East.

I thought that Arabists in the War Office might be impressed by my erudition and, through a thought process no longer recallable, decided that a knowledge of Turkish might impress them even more. I therefore obtained an ancient Turkish grammar, which charmed me with its graceful Arabic script and quaint quotations – I recall one which translated as *A good wine and a pretty woman are two sweet poisons*. But in a more up-to-date textbook I learned that Kemal Ataturk, Turkish dictator and hero of Gallipoli, had completely reformed the language, adopting Roman script and simplifying the grammar. I tried it for a while and was encouraged eventually to buy a biography of Kemal entitled *Grey Wolf*, which titillatingly revealed that he was a syphilitic serial womaniser.

The summons to present myself at the recruitment centre came as a shock. Having abandoned the cloak-and-dagger idea, I'd given little thought to the choice of service apart from ruling out the Navy in the light of Gats's fate. I don't recall discussing the matter with mother Nellie (who probably hoped the whole thing would go away), and although I suppose paternal advice might have been helpful I doubt if Alf's would have differed from most of those who'd survived 'the first lot' – 'Go for a soft job behind the lines, lad, and when you're in never volunteer for anything.'

It was literally on the way to the centre that I decided to opt for the RAF, and as there seemed little point in joining a flying service and remaining earth-bound, to go the whole hog and apply for pilot training – academic, I thought, as it seemed unlikely that I'd pass the medical, being beanpole-thin and having lived under the cloud of a sleeping heart valve (diagnosed by our family doctor following a near-fatal whooping cough bout in early childhood). I'd always half-expected that, Keats-like, I would die young wept over by a circle of grieving girlfriends.

To my surprise I passed the medical A1, was accepted for training as a pilot, and left the recruitment centre with a firm step, consciously straightening my back – which over the last year or so of intense reading had developed the beginning of a monkish stoop.

Again there was delay before the final call to arms, probably because of the overwhelming response to a recruitment drive for aircrew, notable for its successful poster and press recruitment campaign featuring skyward-gazing young men whose glossy Marcel Waves led to aircrew being labelled *Brylcreem Boys*.

To get myself into the military frame of mind I'd thought fit to join the Local Defence Volunteers (soon to be renamed Home Guard and later lampooned as 'Dads Army') where, in a local company of mostly old soldiers, I learned the elements of rifle drill, Morse code and other mysteries of the military calling, and was renowned for sleeping on guard duty, a crime which might have got me shot in Alf's war.

I wasn't sorry towards the end of 1940 to get the final call. Several friends were already in khaki and I was tiring of my role as *rapporteur* of life on the home front. Some of their descriptions of army life were bizarre: rice pudding cooked in tin baths; a sergeant yelling at a recruit on church parade, 'Take your 'at off in the 'ouse of God you stupid bugger'; and the bizarre response of the somewhat unworldly Ronald on finding that the man in the next bunk had suffered a nocturnal bladder failure – 'Look here, you've micturated in my boot!'

As ordered, I reported to the Aircrew Reception Centre (ACRC, Arsey-Tarsey) which had been established at Lord's Cricket Ground near Regent's Park, where there seemed to be thousands gathered on the sacred turf, metamorphosing from variously garbed civilians into uniformly blue U/T pilots or observers, the latter soon to be redesignated 'navigators' – perhaps because it had become difficult to observe now that cockpits were enclosed? White cap-flashes marked us out as the potential elite. I learned that other aircrew such as Wop/Ags were mustering elsewhere.

Accommodation and food were basic. We ate in a large hall belonging to the London Zoo – which raised questions about the meat they served us. As there was no provision for cleaning our issue cutlery (irons) it was the custom to wipe them on the long window curtains near the exit, which led to the rumour that after a while they would be boiled to make soup.

ACRC London – author in second row up, third from the right

We were organised into 'flights' of about forty, each in the charge of a corporal, and told that we were likely to remain together throughout initial training. After some basic drill and much marching we were posted to an Initial Training Wing in Torquay where accommodation was in a requisitioned hotel near the sea front.

It turned out to be a twelve-week course of purely ground training – drill, physical jerks, lectures on basic navigation, meteorology, Morse code, RAF regulations and something called 'airmanship', a code of concepts and conduct enshrining principles laid down by the RAF's founding father 'Boom' Trenchard (so nicknamed because of his loud voice which was said to have echoed through the corridors of the Air Ministry).

The examinations at the end were not difficult – I suppose most of those accepted for pilot training were reasonably well educated – and I don't recall many dropouts. The drill and PT corporals gave us a hard time but by the end of the course had almost become objects of affection, themselves not quite managing to conceal a measure of pride at having turned a collection of unmilitary individuals into a disciplined body of potential aviators.

ITW Torquay – author in centre, Chum on the right

In common with many day-school educated recruits from backgrounds where a degree of privacy in family relations was the norm – and especially in my case, the only male in a fatherless family – I found difficulty in adapting to the all-shower-together ethos which I supposed had spread downwards from public school entrants, and I sensed in the steamy atmosphere a *frisson* which I imagined was homosexual.

One particularly sensitive soul, slender and feminine-handsome, came in for some rough teasing and had his bottom boot-blacked after complaining about drunken behaviour following a rugby match. I made a point of defending him and was rewarded by discovering that like me he was a T.S. Eliot fan. Surprisingly, our habit of quoting at each other after lights-out chunks of *The Wasteland*, *Prufrock* and other half-comprehended gems came to be tolerated — even to some extent enjoyed — by the hearties.

> *I grow old . . . I grow old*
> *I shall wear the bottom of my trousers rolled . . .*

became a sort of incantation on the march, to the mystification of the corporals.

Our seaside surroundings were pleasant and the citizens of Torquay welcoming. One could almost have forgotten the war but for the presence of badly burned RAF officers (including Battle of Britain survivors) convalescing in the city, their shiny facial skin grafts and red-rimmed eyes taking some of the shine off our enthusiasm. A more heartening reminder was the Pearl Harbor attack of 5 December 1941 which brought the United States into the war and instantly transmogrified Yank (an American volunteer) from much-teased apologist to star-spangled hero.

I passed the exams comfortably but am not proud of my behaviour on the last night in Torquay. A walk with the nice girl I'd met some weeks earlier ended in an intimate fumble on a tree-clad embankment leading down to the sea front, halfway through which I suddenly realised that we were missing the end-of-course celebration in a nearby pub. Ungallantly breaking off the engagement, I hurried her along in time to join in the beery singing of that most suggestive of wartime songs:

> *Roll me over in the clover,*
> *Roll me over lay me down*
> *And do it again!*

I've often wondered whether the unsatisfied girl saw the irony of it.

The announcement that before leaving we were to parade for issue with flying kit was welcomed as since call-up there had been neither sight nor smell of an aircraft. Yank voiced the general satisfaction: 'Guess it's about time we were getting our asses strapped to an airplane.'

Little Nell

Flight mates in the smoke-fugged compartment must have wondered at my excitement as the last-lap train from Torquay halted in a flurry of snowflakes at a small station which the guard's shout identified as Desford. 'My granddad and grandma were born here,' I babbled, 'and home's only a stone's throw away.'

Our destination had of course been a secret, and as usual in wartime the journey had been spent in a comatose state dozing, reading and playing brag or twist, so what with the obliterated station names and darkened carriage windows we'd had little idea of our whereabouts.

Desford, a small village in a coalmining area west of Leicester, was distinguished only by its 'aerodrome' and the Industrial School – an early Borstal which I would be threatened with after the twelve o'clock horses which came for you if you didn't go to sleep promptly had lost their power to frighten. Thornton, mother Nellie's native village, was only a few miles away.

'Stone's throw' had been minimising it a bit as our house in Leicester's western suburbs was some seven miles away, but astonishingly it shrank to walking distance when we were immediately transferred from Desford to a satellite field – Braunstone aerodrome, peacetime home of a small flying club whose members were able to drink and perform verbal aerobatics in a nearby pub, *The Airman's Rest*. I telephoned Nellie with the welcome news but had to tell her that it would be a week before I could get home as we were to start flying at once.

It would be a three-week course of basic flying aimed at weeding out anyone who through persistent air sickness, poor coordination or other unairmanlike debility was considered a hopeless prospect for a flying role – and not worth sending to Canada or South Africa under the Commonwealth Air Training Scheme to which we were all looking forward (until America declared war some were trained there disguised as civilians).

My first taste of flying was to be in the rear open cockpit of a dual control Tiger Moth (DH82), the RAF's standard starter biplane in a civil version of which Amy Johnson had flown to Australia in 1930. My instructor, F/O Stanley, was a large, weather-beaten man of middle age who might have been a Great War RFC pilot. He was bluffly kind and patient, even more so when he learned of my local connection as he too was a Midlander and had been a member of the flying club.

It was bitterly cold throughout our stay and, although kitted out with helmet, one-piece gabardine flying suit and floppy suede flying boots, I coveted the fur-lined leather jacket and huntsman-tight boots of my instructor (whose bulk so filled the front cockpit that the view forward was almost obscured). Familiarity with cockpit layout, effect of controls, starting procedure, taxiing, take-off, straight and level flying, climbing and stalling are among the exercises in my training log book, but it was *spinning* which brought realisation of how disorientated a cork must have felt when being removed at speed by the wine waiter in Hollywood films.

As the course progressed the phrase with which all U/T pilots became familiar throughout training – 'Right-o you've got her' – was emerging ever more frequently through the speaking tube, and towards the end I was even allowed to make a glide approach and landing, though I was pretty sure that another hand was on the joystick before touchdown.

As a treat F/O Stanley took me on a low-level flight over Thornton and its surrounds, naming the villages which, under their blanket of snow, brought to mind tales I had often heard of sheep being rescued from drifts in the hard winters of my mother's childhood. As we buzzed the village church I recalled her remark when, during a rare revisitation of her roots soon after Alf had left us, we were gazing at the Ten Commandments writ large in the nave: 'There should be an extra one – *Thou shalt not leave thy wife and kids in the lurch!*'

Before returning to the airfield we skimmed low over the grey surface of Thornton reservoir, Leicester's major water resource and the village's sole claim to distinction. In the past I'd seldom thought of my capable and often hot-tempered mother as a little girl, but this bird's eye view unlocked an early memory of her telling us of climbing the surrounding fence and leading her posse of village children through the trees to the water's edge, a daring exploit in those days when public access to these man-made lakes was strictly forbidden on public health grounds.

Other half-forgotten tales of her tomboy behaviour as the family 'nib' were brought to mind, mostly recalled by my two maiden aunts: climbing trees and tearing her knickers on the branches; and terrorising Nance, her nervous sister, by jumping out at her in the dark just as the poor girl was venturing down the garden to the privy. On one occasion she terrified her father when he was haymaking near the railway by racing across in front of a goods train, he not knowing whether she was alive or dead until the jack-in-the-box (as the guard's van was then known) had gone by, when she shot him a cheeky grin.

One of Nellie's own party pieces was of entertaining her friends by getting Miss Orme, the village shopkeeper, to take down sweet bottles one after another from the topmost shelf, and then deciding that she wouldn't after all spend her ha'penny or farthing. The poor woman had a speech impediment which Nell would round off the performance by mimicking.

Semi Paradise

The weather eased off a little and at the end of the first week I felt at home in the friendly little aircraft, and with F/O Stanley's assurance that I had the making of a pilot I set off for *Greyfell*, if not walking on air at least hopeful that one day wings might sprout on my chest.

The familiar route skirted one of Leicester's vast areas of unrelieved council housing – the Braunstone Estate – built by the city council in the twenties on land acquired by compulsory purchase. Although our house was comfortably beyond the city boundary, with a *cordon sanitaire* of private development between us and the estate, it was always felt necessary to make it clear that *our* Braunstone was freehold country.

If this has a snobbish ring I fear that it reflected the reality of the times, as I learned in July 1943 when 'crewing-up' as second pilot at my first OTU – an informal coming together of pilots, navigators and Wop/Ags, much on the lines of the sounding-out ritual for choosing the leader of the Tory party. I'd approached an NCO skipper, having learned that he was from Leicester and was looking for a second dicky. He seemed quite friendly, but later in the sergeants mess anteroom I overheard him discussing me with those crew members he'd managed to select. 'Don't think he'll do: comes from a bloody great council estate in my town.' I retired hurt but said nothing and soon crewed-up with the experienced flight lieutenant with whom I stayed until becoming a skipper on another squadron. On later learning of the loss with all hands of the aircraft piloted by the man first approached, sympathy was laced with a measure of *Schadenfreude*.

Just beyond Braunstone village, its blacksmith's forge now a car repair garage, I turned my back on well-meaning municipal uniformity and entered the pleasant avenues of inter-war private development which government policy and the spread of those catalysts of cautious capitalism, the building societies, had brought within reach of mother Nellie, father Alf and thousands of other tenants of city terraces.

I was instantly back on my pre-teen paper round, scanning the risible house names, so many of which combined the first owners' forenames in the sort of symbiosis which would see Kenneth and Dorothy enjoying connubial bliss behind *Kendor*, while *Milton* would lend a poetic twist to Mildred and Tony (I often used to wonder what happened when the relationship fractured or the house changed hands).

The most unfortunate combination was the one dreamed up by the parents of my friend Dick, who lived in the next-but-one avenue. He had an elder brother, Harold, so the house had been named *Hardick*. I doubt whether his saintly parents were ever conscious of the *double entendre* which turned out to be oddly prophetic as Dick was a most precocious lad who was rolling the girls in the hay while the rest of us were still making sheep's eyes at them. It was well that he got his experience in early as he too joined the RAF as a pilot and was lost with his crew in a Halifax bomber over the Ruhr.

Not only the houses, but many of the avenues (including ours) were personalised, *Greyfell* being in Edward Avenue which, far from honouring the likes of Victoria's corpulent son or the Prince of Wales (soon to have the nation looking up the word *Abdication* in its dictionaries), was named after the elder son of Mr Kirkland the builder, employed by his father to supervise the work of bricklayers, carpenters, tilers, plumbers and so on, which went on for some time after our arrival as vacant plots were sold.

Mr Kirkland, a brisk moustached and trilbied man of middle age, dubbed the parallel road with the family surname, and as a final gesture of confidence in the quality of his work rounded off the speculation by building for himself a double-fronted detached house with *four* bay windows at the confluence with the main road, living there, so far as I know, for the rest of his life.

This familial naming by speculative builders of the avenues and closes under which they were burying the green suburban fields was not unusual in the twenties and thirties. Grandfather Tom Harrison took a modest jump onto the bandwagon after retiring from tailoring and draping by building a twin row of houses near to his far from modest bungalow and naming the result Dorothy Avenue after his younger daughter. (Later, after father Alf had decamped and relations with his family severed, a pair of houses was gifted to my two aunts, calling forth acerbic comments from Nellie.)

Now, as I entered it from the end which on our arrival in the late twenties had been a cul-de-sac beyond which were cowslip and wild orchid-sprinkled fields, I had a sentimental vision of the avenue as it had been in the pioneer years – eyeless bay windows in half-built houses, plots replete with timber-stack dens and brick redoubts where the cheerful builders would share with us their bacon and bread fried on polished shovels over a brazier as a *quid pro quo* for the hot water provided by our mothers for the mashing of tea brewed in a billy can, leaves glued together with sugar and condensed milk.

Greyfell

Looking at the house name suspended on short chains in the porch I speculated for the hundredth time on the derivation. I'd always thought it was distinctive and must have been chosen by Nellie, though she was always vague about its origin. Alf hadn't the style – or interest – as he himself was semi-detached and probably already plotting the getaway which came about two years after the move.

The bow-shaped bay windows of the house and its Siamese twin still reminded me of a smiling face unlike, for instance, Dick's semi and its neighbour, whose Euclidian square bays had seemed to scowl at their opposite numbers as if accusing the owners of defaulting on their mortgages. I'd always thought that a pair of eyebrow gables would have added the touch of *hauteur* enjoyed by some in the avenue, but accepted that the extra cost would have stretched Alf and Nell too far.

Ten shillings a week is what I believe they paid the Leicester Temperance Building Society for *Greyfell* (which cost £550, on top of which the Government paid the builder a subsidy of something like £100, provided it came up to standard). Grandpa Tom, who had become a local councillor for the rural district in which we lived, was a member of the committee charged with inspecting applicants for the grant, and I remember the chortle as he told of putting his foot through the brick wall of one candidate – who of course was turned down.

Ten bob seems a ludicrously small sum until one realises that five pounds a week was then a comfortable wage for a family man. It loomed larger for Nellie after Alf had finally absconded taking the next week's mortgage money.

Greyfell

My 'woo-hoo' through the kitchen door brought her downstairs from the office-boxroom at speed. 'Just doing the invoices, duck – don't want to miss my discounts!' (She had always left to the last minute settlement of warehouse bills in the credit drapery business rescued from collapse after Alf's departure.)

After a vigorous squeeze I was held at arm's length while she made a careful appraisal. Then it was off with the greatcoat and another inspection. 'I think they've filled you out a bit, and I'm sure you look taller – must be six foot.' (I was five-eleven.) 'Fancy you . . . I never thought . . .' (Her voice broke but quickly mended.) 'You take after your dad in uniform – but, thank the Lord, in nothing much else!'

(I wasn't altogether with her on Alf in uniform. He'd joined the Cameronians soon after August 1914 and the only photographs of him in uniform I've seen show thin, rather feminine legs emerging from his kilt. It was not at all the braw brecht figure of the typical Scotsman, which is not surprising as so far as I know his only connection with north of the border was partiality for a tot of scotch (though beer was his main tipple) which would have commended him to Field Marshall Haig, scion of the firm of whisky distillers and the man who almost succeeded in preventing my existence.)

Alfred in uniform

'I'm ever so sorry, duck, but I've got to nip out for an hour. I missed a couple of customers on yesterday's round and if I don't call today it'll be a few bob to the pub instead of off their accounts. You won't mind, will you? We'll have a panful of eggs and chips when I get back.' I assured her that I'd be happy to get re-acquainted with the house, and anyway wanted to sort out a few books to take back with me.

Mother Nellie on her Raleigh, 1942

While she was putting her coat on – a green-and-tan check with raglan sleeves, worn with a side-slanting tammy (which like most of her clothes she'd made herself) – I wheeled out her bike from the garage, recalling the day when the Raleigh Sports with Sturmy-Archer three-speed had arrived to replace the sit-up-and-beg curved frame model with skirt guard of the kind still seen in Amsterdam. As I waved her off, coat flying in the wind, I thought how stylish she looked.

Returning to the kitchen I poured another cup of now-stewed tea, triggering an olfactory memory of the herbs which she had taken for her 'nerves' during the crisis years following Alf's departure, when the struggle to keep the business afloat was at its most desperate. Mistletoe and valerian were, I seem to remember, basics of the evil brew, the pungent odour of which would linger long in the kitchen, blending with the toxic fumes of the carbide which, reacting with water dripping on it from above, had fuelled the lamp on her old bike. (In a biography of Orson Welles by Barbara Leaming[*] I recently read that his father, a manufacturer of bicycle and automobile lamps in Kinosha, Wisconsin, sold his business *to avoid shifting from the popular carbide lamp he had invented to what he viewed as the newfangled electrical model, because he thought the latter likely to explode on bumpy roads*. Not a lot of people . . .)

As I moved from room to room of the silent house in which the whole of my adolescence and young manhood had been spent, and which I doubted – rightly as it proved – that I would ever inhabit again, I recalled the history of each piece of furniture and every house improvement carried out since our arrival at the end of the twenties.

The light-oak panelling of hall, staircase and landing; the Murphy console radio from which Chamberlain's mournful Sunday morning declaration of war had issued, myself as man of the house comforting a tearful Nellie; the wardrobe of the Queen Anne-style bedroom suite in which, during my absence, Mildred's cat had taken up residence and chewed into confetti to make her bed every one of my airmail letters from Canada, intended as an epistolary diary . . . It was like charting the country's recovery from the consequences of the Wall Street Crash which, as the business picked up after Alf's departure, had given Nellie the wherewithal to exercise her natural taste and flair.

Upstairs, the loft hatch in the landing ceiling was a reminder of the many mischief hours spent alone in the house during adolescence. I'd

---

[*] *Weidenfeld & Nicolson 1985*

discovered that from our roof space I could squeeze past the chimney breast into that of our neighbours' and drop down onto their landing – to explore the house on days when they were 'standing market' at their hosiery stall in Leicester.

The pilfering was petty – a fancy biscuit or two, chocolates from an opened box (which I guessed each would suspect the other of having taken on the sly) – luxuries of which there were few in our penurious years. The real attraction was the drawerful of silk underwear in the marital bedroom, the like of which was not to be seen in *Greyfell*. The burglarious adventures ended when, the day after one of these incursions, Nellie was amazed to learn from Mrs C that a pair of French knickers had apparently walked from the chest of drawers to the double bed.

Some three years before call-up I had accompanied Mr C in his Riley on a trip to Nottinghamshire to pick up stock for the market stall. I'd taken along Lawrence's *Sons and Lovers* and the memory of sitting in the car on a sunny day reading it during his factory calls, surrounded by the mining country of the novel, remains green. In retrospect, I regretted having trespassed on his wife's underwear and there remains a residue of guilt.

The Anderson air raid shelter I'd helped Mr C to install between the two houses triggered a memory of the only opportunity I'd had of experiencing the sort of sexual introduction which always seemed to have been available to youths in French novels or biographies through the ministrations of an experienced woman. It occurred in November 1940 during the blitzing of our neighbouring city, Coventry, when not long after the sirens sounded there was droning from above and Nellie and I, gathering up flask and blankets, joined our neighbours in the shelter.

With them was Mrs C's sister-in-law, relatively young and flashily attractive, who was taking refuge during her husband's absence on Home Guard duty. She squeezed in beside me, adding a welcome whiff of perfume to the shelter's sour dampness, and as the bomber stream developed into a river of pulsating sound we began to take comfort in a close liaison which gave rise to heavy breathing and half-stifled gasps, with 'exploring hands encountering no defence' as Eliot so delicately put it in *The Wasteland* – and minimal underwear.

All in the cringing darkness must have known what was going on, but just as the embarrassment level was becoming almost palpable there was a break in the bomber drone, explained years after the war as a redirection of the stream to ensure maximum damage. Taking advantage of this she asked if I would escort her home – she lived nearby – to collect another blanket, whereupon Nellie, with pointed alacrity, sprang up to fetch one from *Greyfell*.

Whilst I have always regretted that her action almost certainly deprived me of a Mrs Robinson experience I doubt if I would have been any more successful than Dustin Hoffman, though even an attempt would have left imperishable memories. There was no repeat performance – the word must have been passed to her husband who henceforth devoted more attention to guarding his own home, and anyway, as air raid warnings became fewer, we tended to ignore them and the shelter soon reverted to its main function as a drainage sump.

Leicester's Luftwaffe visits were few compared with other targets, though there was one quite prolonged raid in 1940 which found me after office hours in the book room of the County Library in *Grey Friars*, an old part of the city where I was then working, engaged in some unliterary research with a Katherine Hepburn-lookalike librarian. When the sirens forced a break in our activities the inclination was to flee, but on second thoughts we thought it might be safer to stay put and so took refuge at the bottom of the book lift shaft.

We had found some blankets and were quite cosy as the Brock's Benefit of exploding bombs and bursts of anti-aircraft fire started up, though the developing racket was hardly conducive to exploiting the situation to the full. It was not the safest place to be as a direct hit on the building would probably have brought the lift down on top of us ('In death they were not divided'), but fortunately the immediate area went unscathed. At first light we emerged and went our separate ways through the smitten city, though there was little damage in the area through which I pedalled.

Inconclusive as these episodes were, perhaps Adolf should be credited with two tries!

The four flight friends I took to *Greyfell* at the course-end were amazed when Nellie served up enough eggs, chips and bacon to satisfy our wolfish appetites – off-ration spoils from her country customers as *quid pro quos* for reductions in their accounts. Chum, an ex-merchant seaman, pleased me by remarking how young she looked – which at forty-six or so she did (and remained so in my eyes until in her early sixties a series of accidents and a burglary at *Greyfell* seemed to age her overnight). Chum charmed her – his blondly handsome features and broad smile must have been persuasive of his beneficial influence on the son-and-heir. But then she had never been exposed to his recitations of *Eskimo Nell* ('. . . *and forty whores drew down their drawers at Dead Eye Dick's command*') and other classics.

She was surprised to hear me answering to 'Bill'. I explained that Chum had found it difficult to get his tongue round 'Graham', which would come out 'Grim'. I didn't add that I'd anyway thought it a good idea to mark the transformation from bookish boy to man of action by adopting the more manly forename, which I retained to the war's end. Many in the services – men and women – used the cover of the war years to change both manners and expectations, which post-war could make resumption of relationships difficult. I myself succeeded in losing my hard Midlands 'a' for 'ah' though for some time I skated round such solecisms as 'stepping on the gars'.

In Suspension

On the evening before leaving *Greyfell* at first light to brave the U-boat-swarming Atlantic for an absence of what would likely be the best part of a year I was sitting in the twilight with Nellie and Mildred (elder sister Peggy by then married) before a living room blaze which threatened to crack the fireplace tiles, when the phone rang. It was a couple in the next road I'd met at a series of lectures on Beethoven's symphonies asking me round for a last listen to a recording of the *Eroica* before what they predicted would be endless jazz – and 'one for the boat'. At Nellie's urging I went, stayed too long and returned in a fuddled state to a dying fire and Nellie holding back tears. I don't know about conscience making cowards of us all, but it certainly lasts!

Heaton Park, a vast clearing in the Manchester urban rain forest, was the RAF transit camp for those awaiting embarkation to Canada via Liverpool, and it was here that our flight mustered before being allocated to billets in surrounding houses. Each morning we reported to a large building in the park, its otherwise bare interior furnished with row-on-row of seats filling up with hundreds of U/T pilots and navigators waiting to be called for boarding. Once the drafts had been announced and marched off those not called were free for the rest of the day.

It soon became clear that there was a serious blockage in the pipeline with chorus's of 'Why are we waiting?' rippling along the rows until, with discipline on the verge of breakdown, a wingless Wing Commander appeared on a rostrum to apologise for the blockage, taking off with a misquote of Churchill's Battle of Britain encomium:

> *Never in the history of human conflict have so many been buggered about by so few.*

He followed this with a joke about a secret anti-U-boat weapon involving a Sunderland flying boat armed with cans of green paint. On detection of a periscope, the second dicky would pour the paint onto it from nought feet, whereupon the submarine captain would order 'Up!' in the belief that the periscope tip was still submerged. This would be repeated until the vessel was well clear of the water when it would be shot down.

It was bad enough sitting through this performance once. I and two others had to endure it three times as we had been taken off the draft to act as reserves should anyone drop out. No one did, so we were left behind as the band of brothers I'd trained with was marched off never, apart from Chum, to be seen again. I met him in Canada when awaiting return to the UK. He'd failed as a pilot and been commissioned as a bomb aimer, and so was almost certainly destined to become part of Harris's heavy bomber force with no great prospect of survival.

After the war I spotted the name of another flight member, Denys Teare, on the cover of *Evader*,* a very readable account of his adventures after baling out of his bomber over occupied France.

I remember the waiting time until there was a gap in another draft as wet and miserable. Years later, a *Punch* cartoon showing a Manchester bus in London's Piccadilly Circus, with a lone rain cloud above it on an otherwise sunny day, triggered the memory. There was little to do and I missed Chum and the others. The only bright spot was the first showing in Britain of *Citizen Kane* at a local cinema – it so stunned me that I blathered about it to the landlord back at the billet. 'Aye, lad, but has it got a bit of gunplay in it?' was the dry old stick's comment. 'I do like a bit of gunplay.'

Eventually someone dropped out of a draft and I joined a new flight which, having bonded as ours had during initial training, took a little while to accept me. Lofty, a tall ex-milkman was the first to unbend, perhaps because I laughed loudest at his racy tales of 'slipping a crafty 'nana' between the ready thighs of east-end housewives during their partners' absence defending King and Country. Danny, a lowland Scot, became another close buddy, though I had difficulty in penetrating his dense Glaswegian accent.

(I didn't have to persist for long as he was 'washed out' after losing his nerve on the first solo at Elementary Flying Training School (EFTS) in Manitoba – my own nerves shredding as I watched his Tiger Moth circling the airfield before being led down by his instructor.)

The ship we boarded in Liverpool was the *Rangitiki*, an old and battered merchantman known as the Randy Turkey. As our convoy got under way it became clear that this was to be no luxury cruise. Even my modest ambition to sleep in a hammock was frustrated as we dossed down on table tops. Washing was in cold sea water with bars of soap with which one could have built a house, and the only food

---

* *Crecy Publishing*

that sticks in the memory – as it did in my craw – was sugarless, salted porridge.

I turned out to be a good sailor, pacing the deck jauntily as the weaker stomachs committed their contents to the deep. When it wasn't squalling we stood looking down at a huddle of dispirited Luftwaffe POWs in the fo'c's'le, comparing unfavourably with ours their insubstantial grey-blue uniforms (which hardly seemed proof against the Atlantic gales).

We didn't see one aircraft during the two-week voyage, which was not surprising as Coastal Command hadn't yet succeeded in prising more than a token number of long-range aircraft from Bomber Command's Air Chief Marshall Harris, and the recently mobilised United States had yet to get into its aeronautical stride. I don't recall seeing an escort vessel either, though the Navy must have been somewhere in the offing, shepherding our scattered flock. There was no U-boat alert during the passage so we were spared that worst of all spectacles (so familiar from Pathé newsreels) of smoke-billowing tramp steamers up-ending for the final plunge. I remember feeling thankful that I'd joined the RAF rather than the Fleet Air Arm. Apart from the monotony of life at sea there would have been, as Lofty put it, 'Two chances of going for a shit – shot down or shipwrecked.'

There was nothing to do if you weren't a card player or able, as a surprising number were, to sleep the hours away. An uninterrupted read was virtually impossible in our packed and noisy quarters, and the weather was mostly too foul for other than brisk deck patrols, body bent against the wind as in an *Old Persons Crossing* sign.

I had always had the urge to write and now, in a cubbyhole discovered during a prowl below decks – and with the collusion of a friendly crew member – I was left largely undisturbed to fill the inviting blank pages of a part-used Initial Training Wing exercise book with biographical jottings. Although this has long disappeared from among the few mementos of the war years, age has restored the ability to recall in surprising detail names and happenings from the remoter past (at the trivial cost of expunging those of recent years) so that writing the following hasn't been as difficult as expected.

BETWEEN WARS

Beginnings

I first saw the light of day on the eighth of March 1921, though the light was nearly extinguished by the whooping cough bout already mentioned (page 27).

It took Alf six weeks to register my birth, which makes me wonder whether in the interval he'd forgotten the second forename which most children seemed to be burdened with. Stops *en route* to 'wet the baby's head' would have made this more than likely. Perhaps it was a blessing: if the widespread custom of naming a boy after his father had been followed, neither Alfred nor Claude would have suited me.

I have doubts about the reliability of fathers in the birth registration business. When in the sixties I came to obtain probate of my maiden aunt Carrie's will I found that Grandpa Robert Bennett had allowed her forename to be registered not as Caroline, or even Carrie, but *Carry*. Perhaps Robert, then a miner before his graduation to tenant farmer, had noticed the slip when asked to 'sign here' but lost his nerve at the prospect of correcting a man in a suit? I have often wondered.

The house we occupied until the move to the suburbs was in a long respectable street of terraced houses near Leicester's western boundary. It was conveniently close to the tram terminus from which those stately municipal liners departed for the unlovely (but nevertheless beloved) Clock Tower, round which they would pirouette before sailing to intriguing destinations such as Stoneygate (via Gallowtreegate, *shudder!*), Leicester Abbey (where Wolsey expired) and Frog Island.

The earliest years before the clouds of matrimonial dispute gathered are remembered as sunny. Strange, of course, as must be every beginning. Eliot got it about right in *Animula*[*]:

---

[*] *Weidenfeld & Nicolson 1985*

> *'Issues from the hand of God, the simple soul'*
> *To a flat world of changing lights and noise,*
> *To light, dark, dry or damp, chilly or warm;*
> *Moving between the legs of tables and chairs,*
> *Rising or falling, grasping at kisses and toys.*

I didn't have to grasp at kisses. Nellie was a loving mother – and a great storyteller with a penchant for the sadder kind such as *The Little Match Girl* (which usually brought tears when the final Lucifer spluttered out).

Sister Peggy, born in December 1918, was a great doll-lover. She lavished affection on her favourite (which had eyes that opened and shut) so a doll which kicked, cried and needed constant pacifying must have exercised her nascent maternal instinct for longer than normal before jealousy at the attention it was getting from the real mother set in.

The legs of tables and chairs are not so clear in early memories as the twisty legs of a cabinet gramophone. It had double doors guarding a dark tunnel from which issued sounds which I eventually identified as *In a Monastery Garden* (with birdsong trills), *Pique Dame* (Pick-you-dame in Nell-speak), Peter Dawson booming *Glorious Devon*, Amelita Galli-Curci trilling *Lo hear the gentle Lark*, and others, the sounds of which are remembered but their titles forgotten.

The most fascinating object which came to consciousness was a beautifully crafted oak moneybox in the shape of a Great War tank, with guns made from rifle rounds peeping out of the sponsons. Long gone, the memory is always accompanied by a vision of the shiny skin covering the dent in Alf's left temple where shrapnel had penetrated. He never spoke about it, which was typical of most Great Warriors who'd seen action, the only remembered mention of his war being a joke about visiting a neighbouring trench to cadge a few spoonfuls of jam from the occupants who were afterwards blown sky-high, causing his sergeant to grumble: 'Pity you didn't bring the whole jar.'

Of the pictures that swam into my infant vision, the best-loved were three charcoal sketches by Alf, two of dogs and the third an enlarged version of Bruce Bairnsfather's cartoon in which 'Ole Bill' and his comrade, loaded with rifle and pack, are contemplating a flapper who is showing a leg as she darns her underskirt, over the caption: *'Come on Bill, it's safer in the trenches'*. They were sensitively drawn, as were his sketches in autograph books, which were then all the rage. Like Adolf he was a frustrated artist: if only the two could have got together in No Man's Land to talk art during the Christmas 'truce' of 1914 instead of kicking a ball about, twentieth century history might have followed a happier course!

The war was still very much with us. Besides the usual street games of hopscotch, tick and cowboys and indians there was a great emphasis on soldiering. I remember envying older boys standing guard at their entries or marching up and down shouldering dummy rifles – or in the case of a lad named Dudley, an air rifle with which I once saw him shoot a sparrow from his open bedroom window across the street, which brought tears. I was glad when the family emigrated to New Zealand but often wondered what effect Dudley had on the wildlife.

The street was a fairly safe playground with few cars outpacing the horse traffic – which provided nourishment for the tiny front garden of the Misses Winks, a few doors up from us, who would take it in turns to rush out with a shovel and bucket the moment a horse had obliged. Nellie called them 'the Tiddlywinks', either from their habit of popping down to the off-licence in the next street or because their in-and-out routine reminded her of the parlour game.

Next door to them lived Ronald who, although five years my senior, was to become a lifelong friend and mentor after his parents' removal to the western suburbs shortly after ours, but who was rarely seen in the Haddenham Road years. Nellie, half admiringly, half reproachfully, described him as a very clever only child who was kept at his studies so firmly that he had *grown an old head on young shoulders*.

The gramophone, pictures and other treasures were in the front room, which gave onto the street via the tiny privet-hedged garden. Living took place in the back room, which was made snug by a coal-fired range – though cooking was done in the scullery where there was a gas-fuelled oven into which Nellie would occasionally threaten to insert her head during the last stormy years before we moved.

Gas, which powered both heating and lighting with a meter fed by pennies, also featured in an early example of the deceitfulness which Nellie feared I had inherited from Alf, though hoping that an infusion of the Bennett genes would rescue me from outright criminality.

If caught short on change our mother, following the custom of those neighbourly times, would send Peg or me next door to borrow 'a penny for the gas', always promptly repaid. One day, aged five or six, I cottoned on to this as a means of satisfying an overpowering urge to race down to the shop in a neighbouring street and buy a gooey, coconut-topped cornet displayed in the window. I knew it was no use asking Ma (who was always strapped for cash) so I ran round to Mrs Hutchinson next door, borrowed my penny and pelted down to the shop.

I was just sinking my teeth into the sweetmeat when I observed Nellie bearing down on me, her face a mask of menace. She caught me by the ear, ground the cornet into the pavement and marched me home where I was made to apologise to 'Grandma Hutchibobs' (Nellie was Harribobs), who must have twigged the deception, after which I was sent to bed supperless.

Progressively, as the marital bond weakened under Alf's neglect of the credit drapery business inherited from his father, the lengthening absences and the drink (though I don't remember having seen him 'the worse for drink' – or the better, either!), the picture darkened, and Nellie's raging against him could be frightening. One outburst, occasioned by some bad behaviour on my part while Alf was on one of his trial runs, ended with my enraged mother 'backing the fire' with part of a train set discarded by a cousin. The toys were retrieved, blackened and bent, when the raving ended in tears. How she expected metal to burn was a puzzle, solved when I witnessed the charred remains of crashed aircraft during the war.

The worsening marital relationship was not helped by the occasional visits of Grandma Harrison, who would descend on us with my two aunts, bringing a whiff of high life into the living room where they would seat themselves carefully on the edge of their chairs while tea and cake were served. Their visitations couldn't have been enhanced by my behaviour. A mixture of shyness and excitement would drive me under the table from where, cloaked by the oversized chenille tablecloth, I would dart out and attack their legs, barking like a dog.

Nellie & Alf's wedding, 1918

I remember the atmosphere as frigid. Our mother was a proud woman and felt she was being patronised. She blamed both grandparents for not coming clean about their son's pre-war habits which hinted at a drifting kind of youth, and as the years went by much of her bitterness against him was redirected to them.

Although a 'mother's boy' I was fond of Alf, who was kind in a detached way and by no means violent – the sort of husband who would ride the storm of his wife's wrath, a breakwater on which it would spend itself. I can recall only two occasions on which he physically chastised me – the first when I was very slow getting up for school, the second when he caught me caressing the bared bottom of Peg's friend from across the road as we lay sunning ourselves on the patch of grass in the small back garden.

One odd but clear memory . . . If after nightfall I was playing in the street or peering through the modest front room bay window I could always spot his approach by the distinctive soldierly walk and glowing tip of his bobbing cigarette.

Another memory is of the second-hand Citroën which suddenly appeared, behind whose huge steering wheel Sonny sat 'driving' on Alf's knee. There is a dim memory of accompanying him on the country round, sitting in the car with a bag of crisps while he and a drinking pal dropped into a pub to invest some of the takings. The car remained just long enough for Nellie to obtain her licence, which absolved her from the requirement to take a driving test for the Triumph Mayflower she acquired after the war, so that her potentially lethal habit of taking up the whole carriageway when overtaking went uncorrected.

I have often wondered to what heights of middle-class aspiration Nellie might have raised us if blessed with an even moderately ambitious partner. As it was, once Alf had up-anchored and sailed out of our lives she managed through years of struggle to keep *Greyfell's* roof over our heads, and see Peg and I through fee-paying grammar schools and Mildred through secretarial college. When deserted, she was still an attractive woman and could easily have remarried, instead of which she pitched into salvaging the business and looking after us so that we were never saddled with a stepfather, wicked or otherwise.

There were rows, reconciliations, departures and reappearances until one day, when I was about nine, an absence prolonged itself to infinity and Alf never crossed our threshold again, although he and I were destined to meet many years later, with revelations to follow.

Ellen Bennett (Nellie), the author's mother, 1915

Reluctantly to School

The memories of early schooling are confused since Leicester's primary education pattern seemed to be suffering from transitionitis at the time and I was shunted between four schools from age five to eleven. Doubtless, our move from city to county and the effects of boundary changes contributed to this.

My first school was a Victorian red-brick building of two stories, twenty minutes walk from home, intimidating with its shiny green-and-cream painted walls, large high-ceilinged classrooms and echoing corridors. The sharpest memory is of two female teachers bending over me admiring the model of a lorry I'd been making from matchboxes. This had two characteristics – it was more ambitious than the efforts of my classmates and it was never finished. I have always considered this to have been an early indication of my character – full potential limited by lack of persistence.

At the next school, a wooden structure hastily erected to cater mainly for the children on the burgeoning Braunstone Estate, I was charmed by Miss Sturman who escorted me to the hospital after I'd cut my knee rather badly in the playground. I played the brave soldier so well as the stitches were inserted that she bought me two ounces of toffee. But the first female I lost sleep over was a pretty, golden-haired girl named Eileen Boocock, though I couldn't understand how so exquisite a creature could have both a funny surname and a monkey-faced brother.

Next, I was parachuted into another red-brick fortress – Hazel Street School, hard by Filbert Street, home of the City Football club and surrounded by other nutty thoroughfares – Chestnut, Walnut, Brazil . . . Memories of this episode are unhappy because of the charged atmosphere at home as the Alf-Nellie relationship wound down. Peggy was in a senior, all-girls class, and I remember my discomfiture at having to go upstairs with a message for her teacher Mr Marriott, a small man with a bald patch which the girls called a 'fly's skating rink'. With an elder sister's cruelty Peg led her class in an outbreak of giggling as I scurried from the room.

The author with his sisters, Mildred and Peggy

The final stage of elementary education came after we had moved to *Greyfell*, beyond the city boundary and so under the county education authority. Head of my new school was briskly progressive Mr Bradley, whose routine introduction of bad jokes at morning assembly probably implanted the punning virus in this particular pupil. One I remember: 'Why is marmalade so called?' Answer: 'Because when her son praised the home-made orange preserve she replied, "Well, have some *more m'lad!*" It was here that I sat the equivalent of the eleven-plus, which I failed – not surprisingly in view of the number of moves and the home situation.

School attendance, always erratic, became more so after Alf's disappearance. I can do no better than reproduce a piece I wrote a few years ago when truancy was in the news – and sent to the education supplement of one of the broadsheets which promised to publish it but never did:

Truancy Now and Then

It was the milk roundsman who did for me in the late twenties – an alert man in a beige sort of smock, always whistling as he swung through the gate after calling on nice Mrs Elson whose husband was away a lot. Or his cheerfulness could have been relief at the dairy having converted from loose to bottled milk which I'm sure happened at about that time. This would have made his job less back-aching – and much quicker as bottles could be left on the doorstep of those unresponsive to knock or ring. And more time for observation, which was the cause of my downfall.

'Hope Graham'll soon be better, Mrs H,' he cheerfully hoped one morning.

'There's always room for improvement, though he's not a bad lad,' replied mother Nellie. Then, thoughtfully: 'How do you mean, better?'

'You know – back at school.'

I'd like to think that my erstwhile pal whose ladling skills I'd once admired felt a twinge of guilt at the gaffe.

And that's how my fortnight or so haunting parks, building sites and other extra-mural alternatives to school came to an end. No more weekday fry-ups on the polished shovels of brickies and carpenters who were covering the green fields with semis like ours. Or – and I suppose this may have come as something of a relief – any further need to think up credible entries for my fictitious school diary.

Our father, a Great War veteran, had recently absconded, leaving mother with three of us to bring up, so I don't recall the consequences as being too serious. I suppose the junior school head would have been understanding. 'Broken home' they would call it now, though it seemed all of a piece to me and I daresay we were better off without the rows.

I've never understood how I got away with it for so long. Previous odd absences had been picked up by the school attendance officer, a thin-lipped man in a hard hat like a French kepi. Perhaps he was truanting too – not long afterwards he left his wife for a younger woman and disappeared.

It turned out alright in the end. I missed the scholarship but Nellie, bless her heart, stumped up the modest fees for grammar school. I spent most of the war years in the RAF and never went AWOL.

But all strength to those who are trying to stem the rising tide of truancy. One hopes that as part of their strategy they are harnessing the sharp eyes of the milkman, local shopkeeper and community policeman. Of course the last two are a bit thin on the ground these days, what with supermarketing and fast car policing, though thank God the milkman looks like going on for ever. Though I wonder . . . More and more people do seem to be lugging cow juice home in two- or four-litre plastic containers these days.

I must have pulled myself together after the truancy phase as I managed with Nellie's help to gain entrance to one of the four Leicester boys' grammar schools – as a fee-payer. Poshest was the Wyggeston (rugger and a termly fee of six guineas) attended by the remarkable Attenborough brothers – and Dick of *Hardick*. The fees would have been well beyond Nellie's means and anyway Phil, a recent friend, had been a year at City Boys (soccer and two guineas) and seemed to be doing well. So application was made.

At the interview with Mr Crammer, the headmaster, I could see that Nellie's natural taste in both dress and manner was creating a good impression. When asked about my reading habits, ignoring her eye signals, I started by describing stories of Morgan the Mighty and the

Black Sapper in the weekly *Rover* which Phil handed on to me. Mr Crammer must have appreciated his education in the lower reaches of literature because shortly afterwards came a letter offering me a place.

The Great Schism

The prospect of five years of fees must have made even Nellie pause, especially as Peg was already at a girls' grammar school as a fee-payer. But Nellie was Nellie and didn't see her son-and-heir leaving school at fourteen to man a lathe in the British United Shoe Machinery factory, or even to learn the relatively new art – pioneered I believe in Leicester – of making men's half-hose with elasticated yarn so that they would stay up without suspenders.

During a visit to *Greyfell* Grandpa Harrison offered to pay the fees – which he could well have afforded – doubtless feeling that this would be some recompense for siring so unsatisfactory a husband and father. Although Nellie had always had a soft spot for 'Alf's Dad' – and he respected her business acumen – all her resentment at the attitude of the distaff side spilled out at what she regarded as this ultimate attempt to undermine her independence. The offer was declined, both lost their tempers, and after a huge row Grandpa stormed out with some such Parthian shot as: 'Well, then, you can paddle your own canoe and be damned.' That ended all communication between them – they never met again and we children added our paternal grandparents and a couple of aunts to a lost father.

I don't think Nellie ever regretted her decision. She was unsuited for the role of poor relation and must have felt that freedom from the visits of Grandma and her acolyte daughters was worth the loss of Tom. The effect of the breach on me was more profound as from the time of Alf's final disappearance I'd spent many weekends at *Hillsborough* and become something of a favourite with both grandparents and Dolly, younger of the two aunts.

Grandpa had swum into my childhood as a successful tailor and outfitter with a shop in Leicester's west end – our end. Brisk, humorous, smartly dressed – usually with a flower in his lapel – his custom when going into town of taking a hat from the shop window and replacing it on his return I thought wickedly cheeky. Nellie, half admiringly – and puzzlingly to my young self – described him as 'a self-made man', which many years later I heard a Church of England canon define as 'One who thus relieves the Lord of a grave responsibility'. Decisive himself, Tom's description of a ditherer – 'He's like a wooden man made of smoke!' – also puzzled me, though it seemed to make a sort of sense.

Nellie, whose own family was more worthy than wealthy, was inclined to question the origin of the family fortune. The war, whilst ending millions of lives, had *made* many of those on the home front who possessed the heart and energy to take advantage of the opportunities offered. It was said that Tom had prospered from the number of mourning suits supplied to relatives of 'the fallen' as even the poorest strove to observe the full funereal formalities in those days.

What the picture was before 1914 is unclear, though there is some evidence that his origins were more obscure than his wife's, whose family background was farming in South Wales. All I know is that a year or so after the armistice he retired and built *Hillsborough*, a fine bungalow about three miles from our eventual home in the suburbs. This boasted a central bay window more than twice the length of those at *Greyfell*, looking out onto a long front garden dominated by a pedestal-mounted silver globe which reflected the sun so dazzlingly that it had once caused the driver of a car passing along the main road to lose his concentration and mount the wayside verge.

The meteoric rise in his fortunes was symbolised for me by his enjoyment of the occasional breakfast bowl of bread and milk in preference to the grapefruit with which Grandma and Dolly would return from town after a visit to Leicester's posh grocers, Simpkin & James.

There were two daughters. Orpha, the elder, had always seemed to me as strange as her name, which I believe had a biblical origin. Slightly mannish with gingery hair (she would have said auburn) and a quizzical expression, she was married to Will, who travelled in the 'leather trade', which Nellie always spoke of with a certain awe as being a source of great earnings. Soon after his return from a business trip to the USA I made a cheeky remark which earned me his undying hatred. He'd been swanking about his sharp 'Boston haircut' when I piped up cheekily, 'Well it dun't look much different to mine,' which set Grandpa chuckling. On a later holiday in Bournemouth with the grandparents, aunts and Will, I launched into the waves the new clockwork steamboat Grandpa had bought me, where it was lost. There was some sympathy, though none from Will. 'You might as well have bunged the money in the sea,' was his dour contribution. It was left to Grandpa with his touch of humour to buy me the replacement *submarine*. Undying are the memories of adult unkindnesses to children!

Dolly, my favourite, was unmarried, though she was courting during the period leading up to the break with the grandparents (which was around my eleventh birthday). A pleasant woman in her late twenties, she was attractive in a sporty way, regarding the world myopically from behind thickish spectacles. Jim, her 'young man', a tennis playing bank clerk, would appear now and then. Perhaps I was jealous of him because I would irritatingly lurk about during their snatched moments of tenderness ('spooning' in Nell-speak). They married in the early 1930s, neither they nor Orpha and Will producing children, perhaps put off by Alf's poor showing.

Part of the weekend routine at *Hillsborough* would see me mowing the lawns and doing odd things – some very odd, like throwing aloft a home-made parachute, weighted with a stone, and watching it crash through the greenhouse roof to land among Grandpa's prize begonias. The custom was that on Monday morning in term time Dolly would usher me into the grandparental bedroom where they would be sitting up enjoying *Teasmade* cuppas. There I would be presented with sixpence for the weekend tasks before catching the bus, she to work at a city department store, I to school with a slice of Victoria sponge cake (her speciality).

Although *Hillsborough* weekends were some relief from the sometimes-fraught *Greyfell* atmosphere (before Peg's marriage she and Nell, both strong characters, were often at daggers drawn) they were in some subtle way unsatisfying. There was no one to play with and the only books were a few unreadable Sunday school prizes – nothing as nourishing as *Tarzan of the Apes*, *Swiss Family Robinson* or *The Last Abbott of Glastonbury*, favourites among the contents of our glass-fronted bookcase.

Paternal grandparents & the garden globe (note the work boots)

All the same, there remained a residue of regret at my exodus from this land of promise, and whilst in Canada, having in mind the somewhat dubious prospect of survival as an aspiring fighter pilot, I had the impulse to drop a friendly line to Grandpa describing the more amusing sides of flying. I'd always been able to make him laugh with my cheeky sense of humour – on one occasion expressing the hope when they were about to embark on a cruise that they wouldn't find it too rough crossing the *Bay of Whisky*. I never received a reply and rightly guessed that, like many wartime letters, it had gone astray.

On leave shortly before my marriage in May 1944, I conceived the notion of making a surprise visit to *Hillsborough* to introduce my fiancée and proffer the olive branch in person. Nellie was more than dubious. 'They'll think you've gone over looking for a wedding present – that's the sort of people they are.' She was right. The two aunts were in attendance and an unhealthy-looking Will skulked off after the introductions. Grandma, noticing my Flight Sergeant's stripes and crown, made a point of informing me that Dolly's husband Jim was now a Royal Navy officer based at Dartmouth ('Sailing an office desk' – Nellie).

Grandpa, after confirming that he had indeed replied to my letter, murmured that he would send a wedding present. None came – perhaps he had a conscience about it because he left me £200 in his will. Not much for a wealthy man, though it came in handy to pay for my post-war articles as a trainee solicitor. Peggy and Mildred received nothing, but firmly ruled out any thought of my splitting it.

Mr Crammer's Seat of Learning

I was glad of Phil's company on my first day at the new school, having instantly changed from a tousled-haired pleb in jersey and shorts to a toff in black blazer and cap with griffon badge. Overawed initially by the masters in gowns sweeping through the corridors and prefects lording it at morning assembly, I soon settled down and began to enjoy the new life – including a first fight in the playground, with a boy who in the well-worn tradition then became a friend.

Although Latin and Greek were still taught, the emphasis had recently shifted to modern languages, and it was on French (and later German) that I was launched. I've never really regretted this and can just about manage to make sense of inscriptions on tombs and heraldic devices. It was easy to divert Johnny Jeeves, the French master, from irregular verbs to his Great War experiences at Wipers and the Somme.

In the early years I was in a fairly high stream, but my maths, particularly algebra, was weak and no amount of coaching from Peggy – bright in all departments – could make me understand quadratic equations or calculus. She was not the most patient of tutors and sessions would mostly end in a shouting match.

Maths lessons were a torture – the master was a cadaverous man named Carter who had an almost invariable routine involving myself and another Harrison, a pale-faced polymath who I believe went on to enjoy a fairly distinguished academic career. Carter, seeking the answer to a problem on the blackboard, would direct his glare from one to the other of us and then enunciate, 'Harrison,' (pause) 'of the G variety,' whereupon I would totter to my feet and stand mute while the class giggled. After a significant silence I would be told to sit down, whereupon Harrison J F C would trot out the sickly smooth answer. In the end it got so bad that on occasions when I had lunch at the maiden aunts I would fake illness if there were an afternoon maths lesson. It never worked.

I digress for a moment: on a recent re-reading of Richard Hoggart's *The Uses of Literacy*[*] I noticed for the first time that J F C's name appeared in the list of acknowledgements of those who had given 'extensive, detailed and ungrudging help in the preparation of the book'. I wrote to Richard with a copy of this passage but sadly his death was announced a few days afterwards.

Gradually, as the years slipped by, I floated downstream and spent a last comfortable year in a small 'remove' form under the aegis of Bud

---

[*] *Pelican Books 1965*

Fisher, a pleasantly rotund teacher who didn't trouble us too much so long as we gave him a quiet time.

My behaviour throughout was erratic, reflecting I suppose, lack of conventional discipline. I was good at art, English and the two foreign languages, and although not keen on formal sports enjoyed some success as a cross-country runner, perhaps because there were opportunities for disappearing half-way round the course (which was not far from home).

I remember speaking for the motion 'If ignorance is bliss, 'tis folly to be wise' in a school debate, citing the belief in Father Christmas as an example of blissful ignorance. But my moment of true fame came with the approach of one November 5th when I volunteered to give a talk to the school Science Society on making fireworks, with a demonstration.

Like many boys in those days Phil and I possessed chemistry sets and had achieved some skill in making chrysanthemum fountains, Bengal lights and other sparkling pyrotechnics to supplement the modest collection of bought fireworks like rockets, Roman candles and Catherine wheels which were beyond our skills. But in spite of many efforts, our great ambition to make bangers had never been realised – the opening fizzle refused to be the prelude to an explosion.

Having decided that a pyrotechnic demonstration without a big bang finish would be like an overture with no opera I worked away at the recipe. This involved much compression of the chemical mixture within the casing, but in spite of many attempts success eluded me. Suppressing my Bennett genes I finally bought a tuppeny thunderflash to hold in reserve, camouflaging it under layers of brown paper to give it the amateur appearance of the rest. When, after the last chrysanthemum fountain had spluttered to a finish, my homemade explosive went off – not with a bang but a fizzle – I immediately lit the substitute, which of course performed superbly to general acclamation. Hastily, I gathered up the shreds before onlookers could examine the evidence.

This was the peak of my reputation as a scientific guru, and the low mark on my morality scale.

When it came to the school leaving examination I sat pipe-puffing into the small hours, straining but ultimately failing to unlock the meaning or purpose of algebraic equations, and managed to scrape through, gaining my School Certificate (though with only two special credits – in Art and English).

My Leicester burr was smoothed slightly during the final year when an attractive Irish elocution teacher, Miss O'Driscoll, appeared. Sure, she stole our hearts away and some of the masters smartened themselves up, though Mr Pedley (who eventually succeeded Mr Crammer as head) still arrived – appropriately on his bike – with trousers screwed into socks.

When Nellie made her final visit to the school for the leaving ceremony Mr Crammer, no doubt expressing the opinion that I could have done better, told her that had the school been aware of her circumstances and the lack of a father's presence my somewhat erratic behaviour would have been better understood and more might have been done to correct it. A benevolent and good man.

I still have the bible presented to me on leaving and sometimes, in reminiscent mood, I read again the signatures and 'good wishes' of masters and prefects on the title page. They do not include Mr Carter's.

Influential Friends

Wrestavon was the name, teetering on the brink of *Dunromingdom*, of the unpretentious bungalow standing well back from the main road near the city boundary in which my new friend Phil lived with father, step-mother and two older brothers. It had been designed and partly built by father Dick, a retired school attendance officer, whose meagre pension perhaps excused the building's flat refusal to break out into a single bay window, or countenance even the possibility of a future garage by leaving space for one.

My friendship with Phil was of the chalk and cheese variety, the attraction of opposites, symbolised in memory by the precise way in which he rolled up his summer shirt-sleeves so that they would stay put no matter what activity we were pursuing, whereas mine would flop down constantly however hard I tried to do likewise. I suppose each found the other's personality traits mildly irritating, but I believe my more open character 'brought him out', and the association with him and his family introduced me to practical skills and disciplines which Alf had never instilled and Nellie could rarely find time to teach me.

Author (on left) with Phil and his cousin, Mary

What we had in common was the spirit of adventure which at weekends and during school holidays would take us on day-long walks into the countryside beyond the avenues, most often along a gated 'White Road' which snaked over the fields for some miles to the largely notional Leicester Forest East, ending at the village of Kirby

Muxloe (whose ruined castle and pleasant main street belied its manurial moniker). We would return in season with cobnuts, blackberries, field mushrooms and – on one occasion – specimens of a squadron of large buzzing insects discovered hovering over a brackish stream in imitation of the autogyros which were making rare appearances in the Midlands skies. After summer's end, collecting deadwood for the enormous Guy Fawkes bonfire in *Wrestavon's* long back garden would occupy us for weeks.

We also took to camping in a big way, the bell tent bought second hand for a fiver being capacious enough to have slept twenty boy scouts toe-to-pole. Initially pitched near the signal box on the railway line bordering my Uncle Harry's farm at Hugglescote, a small settlement not far from Nellie's native village, we were often joined uninvited at our camp fire by the signalman, a quare fellow, all fluttering hands and shrill laughs – probably homosexual though we wouldn't have recognised it as such in those innocent days. On what turned out to be one wet weekend Nellie and Mildred joined us, and I recall Harry pleading with his sister to abandon the tent for a farmhouse bed as the clouds gathered, but still a nib she declined, later declaring that the night's canvas-lashing downpour had been a great adventure.

Later, Phil and I became more adventurous, during one summer holiday taking the train to Mablethorpe on the Lincolnshire coast (tent and other equipment lugged into the aptly-named luggage van) where we pitched it among the sand dunes. Returning from long walks along the miles of seashore, our trophies, mainly of unusual shells, would also include spent rounds of ammunition fired short by aircraft practising their marksmanship on floating targets – though with only Middle Eastern insurrections in mind since the Daily Express had ruled out any more widespread conflict.

Wrestavon's unremarkable furnishings were enhanced by a respectable collection of books including Shakespeare's plays and volumes of Royal Academy illustrations. In the course of trying everything, father Dick had passed through an oil painting phase, though with less success than in his outdoor activities. Wooden cows ruminated glumly in gloomy landscapes on most of the walls, no match for the sugary nudes in the RA volumes.

From the moment of acceptance I was one of the family and spent an increasing amount of my spare time with Phil making models – mainly boats which we sailed on the backwaters of the sluggish Soar – in the large garden shed with its workbench, lathe and every kind of tool necessary for carpentry and metalwork. The three boys had been reared on the *Boys' Own Paper*, a legendary publication for the adventurous and practical, and although Phil had regressed to *The Rover* the skills were still with him.

Such knowledge as I possess of plants, fruit trees and the rotation of vegetable crops comes from Dick who had mastered the arts of gardening, apiary (I still see him in his Ascot-style hat and veil!), greenhouse construction and tomato and marrow cultivation, with surplus produce on sale at the front gate.

Perhaps more significantly, it was from Dick that I got my socialism, though there was a good deal of anti-Toryism about anyway during the years of unemployment following the Great War. Looking back I see him as the typical product of a brand of left-wing politics peculiar to Leicester – *sensible* socialism, firmly grafted onto cooperative root stock, the city having been a pioneer in setting up producers' cooperatives, which seemed then as now to be a realistic alternative to rampant international capitalism.

A practical supporter of the local branch of the Labour Party, he could be as hard on any member letting the side down as on the opposition. He always referred to the Tories as *Stinkers*, and on graduating from parish to rural district council – of which by that time Grandpa had become chairman – he had on many occasions to bite his tongue when some of the cost-cutting policies which Tom and his fellow Stinkers were espousing appeared on the agenda. I based 'Stratus' Day, a character in my novel *The Last Alderman*,[*] on him and (with apologies for self-indulgence) reproduce an excerpt which, *sans* the epithet, could have been Dick speaking:

---

[*] *Barry Rose Publishers 1975*

You post-war socialists are a poor lot, Sydney. I'd built this party up from nothing — and I could do it again. It's principles you want, Sydney. If you're out you've got to fight your way back — with principles. You're all in it now for what you can get. No better than those bloody Stinkers.

It isn't easy to put a finger on the point at which the friendship between Phil and I began to fragment but I think it must have been soon after he took up tennis at courts near Aylestone, an undistinguished village which Herbert Bowden, Commons Leader and Minister in Harold Wilson's post-war administration, took for his title on ennoblement — unwisely, as it turned out, as those who thought him a bit of a hard case dubbed him Lord Hailstone.

Among the set Phil joined was a girl from one of the posher grammar schools to whom I'd recently sent a *billet-doux*, heavily scented with Peg's *Californian Poppy*, inviting her to a Sunday afternoon's boating on the river which, as I'd realised the moment after pushing it through her letter box, I could in no way have afforded. The news of her laughing refusal filtered through the avenues and must have caused amusement among the tennis friends with whom Phil continued to consort. From then on the sight of his white-clad figure striding towards the courts came to symbolise the parting of the ways.

I suppose our friendship was anyway past its prime, and by then — it would have been mid-1939 — I had begun to see a good deal of Ronald, the studious son of our near neighbours in the City who had also joined the suburban diaspora and now lived in their superior semi almost opposite to, and subtly diminishing, much-loved *Wrestavon*.

Much loved and much regretted. Visiting my roots some years ago after Phil's comparatively early death, I found that it had been demolished to make way for an extension to the adjoining small garage and service station, which in the event had never taken place. Gone! House, garden, greenhouse . . . and with them all physical evidence of the better part of boyhood.

Graham and Ronald – Victoria Park, Leicester, 1939

Ronald, though he shared my aversion to tennis and sport generally, followed the cricket scores and would, at odd intervals during the walks we began to take together, punctuate his attempts to enlighten me on some aspect of the metaphysical and religious writings of Rousseau and D'Alembert with a phantom stroke to square leg or silly mid-on (wherever that was).

He'd recently surfaced from long immersion in the waters of academe – which had earned him first-class honours in French at Leicester University College (whose principal was Attenborough *père*), followed by a year at the Sorbonne studying the enlightenment philosophers, and ending with a stint at Oxford for a diploma in education. Now he was to be seen in college blazer with open-neck shirt ('glad neck' in Nell-speak) walking somewhat absent-mindedly to or from the bus terminus, usually with a clutch of library books, constantly greeted by neighbours who, instead of the pallid bookworm they'd half-expected, were confronted by a well-built, fair-complexioned young man of twenty-three who seemed quite willing to stop and chat.

Ours was an odd coming together. I'd seen virtually nothing of him since early childhood. In those days his impression of me could only have been of an untidy hoop-rolling street Arab, indistinguishable from the rest – unless spotted in the palmy days before the marriage began to crumble, when Nellie would toff me up for outings in an all-white outfit (shoes, socks, shorts, shirt and cap – a scowling, junior Great Gatsby).

I was by now reasonably presentable in the sports-coat-and-flannels youth uniform of the late thirties, had kept up and enhanced my French and German, and was an omnivorous if somewhat random reader. Above all, I was ripe for intellectual stimulation of the kind which Phil had been unable to provide.

Before their move to the suburbs Ron's parents had kept closed house to protect their son's need for uninterrupted study. Now that his scholastic life was well launched they could let up somewhat, and perhaps also, like most of the suburban diaspora, had a wish for the world to witness their improved circumstances. There may also have been some feeling of guilt on their part at the Trappist years they'd imposed on their son. At any rate, they seemed to approve of our budding friendship and readily admitted me to the laager.

In parallel, Nellie and Mrs G struck up an edgy kind of relationship. She was, in my mother's phrase, 'a bit of a tartar', and I too found her rather formidable, identifying her with the *Mammon of*

Righteousness, a dominating mother in one of PC Wren's stories. Not one for hiding the family light under a bushel, she would be pounced upon by Nell for her occasional bouts of boasting. On one occasion, hearing the good lady declare in company that, 'Of course I send all our washing to the laundry!' Nell, recalling that they had recently acquired a washing machine, chipped in with, 'So what do you use the Bendix for?' 'Oh – just to wash the dusters,' replied the quick thinker. This exchange, elaborated on each telling, became one of Nellie's party pieces.

Husband Herbert, a quiet man who struggled to keep up with his clever son, seemed to have retired from regular employment, but kept the large gardens, front and rear, in prime condition. I have the image of kindly Herbert joining us in the front room to make what he could of the music we were listening to on the radiogram. This would more often than not have been Brahms (Ron's favourite composer) or Sibelius, the hesitant opening theme of whose second symphony, hummed with pounding fist accompaniment by Ron soon after the start of our friendship, was responsible for my Damascene conversion from the trotting tunes of dance music and light jazz to the heavy horses of the full symphonic range. He must have been gratified by this, though perhaps a little alarmed by the speed at which I raced ahead from Sibelius to Bartok, Stravinsky, Schoenberg and Weburn, by-passing much of Beethoven, Mozart, Schumann and Co – to be mopped up later.

Some of the mopping up was accomplished when I attended a course of lectures by Leicester's Cathedral organist and choirmaster on Beethoven's symphonies, all nine analysed in some depth with the aid of 78 rpm records, so that even today I subconsciously mark the point at which the sound was abruptly suspended.

Maisie, a pretty blonde girl, joined the Beethoven class when we were about to romp through the Pastoral symphony. As she lived in my direction I began to walk her home, and by the light-hearted Eighth we were making such intimate music together in the dark entry of her terraced house that I invited her to *Greyfell* on an evening when Nellie would be out on the round until late. 'Can't possibly,' she trilled, 'Friday night's *Amami* night!' The choral Ninth and my aversion to liaising further with a shampoo advert ended the budding romance.

In what memory tells me was the last pre-war summer, Ron and I took to walking tours of the city, during which I came to suspect that his year in Paris may not have been entirely spent cooped up in the Sorbonne. Had he, I wondered, been a bit of a *boulevardier* in his unbookish moments? As we strolled through the avenues of Stoneygate and Knighton in the posher parts of the city he exhibited a flair for engaging likely-looking girls in conversation of a flatteringly erudite flavour which almost hinted at the *flâneur*. My outsize pipe, like a destroyer making smoke, was useful as an icebreaker and I had my own line of *badinage*.

Betty in her National Fire Service uniform

It was on one of these forays that I met the girl who was to become my wife. She was walking the family dog, and they made a striking couple. We both thought her rather special, but Ron was called early to the colours and so it was I who was able to pursue the long campaign which (with Nellie's whole-hearted approval and connivance) ended in victory just a year before D-Day.

Toading

I left school at sixteen: no question of staying on for 'Higher Schools' and university. Phil had left the year before to embrace the old toad work (as Larkin[*] called the nine-to-five life sentence) and now had a job with the city council. Father Dick strongly recommended a local government career. 'You won't make your fortune but if you work hard and take your exams there'll be regular promotion and a pension at the end.' With Nellie's approval I began to comb the ads in the *Leicester Mercury*, influenced more by the prospect of life among the attractive girls I'd witnessed tripping in and out of the town hall than a pension. On spotting an advert for an administrative job in the County Council headquarters – thought to be a cut above the town hall – I applied and was called for interview.

For a junior clerkship at ten shillings a week I expected to be quizzed by a minor official, but no! It was into the large, law book-lined office of the County Clerk himself that I was ushered – Mr Lucas Eustace Rumsey, a middle-aged, silver-haired solicitor of some presence who quickly put me at my ease. I interviewed well and was offered the job.

Nellie was relieved that her ambition to see me in a suit rather than overalls had been achieved, and was impressed when my first month's salary was paid by cheque, though commenting that it was so small as to be hardly worth the paper it was written on.

The Council headquarters then occupied an imposing building at the junction of Friar Lane and Grey Friars, part of old Leicester '*where the Cathedral rears its lofty spires*', as with artistic licence I

---

[*] *The Whitsun Weddings*, Faber & Faber Ltd 1964

later put it in a mock epic inspired by Pope's *Rape of the Lock*, which we'd studied at school:

> *And where the lordly Lucas reigns on high*
> *Cosseted by the nymphs of county squires*

many of whom were indeed the daughters of Leicestershire worthies, products of secretarial colleges, there to earn pin money and possibly click with an eligible lawyer or other up-and-coming staff member.

The pillared portal of the Council building opened onto a wide entrance hall from which steps led to upper floors, all in terrazzo 'marble'. In a recess on the left of the hall was the Enquiry Office, an open area containing the telephone switchboard, with a long counter to keep the public at bay, which is where I would be starting.

It turned out to be a good introduction to the administrative machine. Presiding over it, wizard of the switchboard and fount of knowledge, was Jim, a shortish man in his thirties with a sardonic sense of humour and a body badly deformed by childhood tuberculosis. He was intelligent, not one to suffer fools gladly, and able to take liberties with even senior people who (if they were wise) would listen to his advice on matters of protocol: 'I don't think you really want to see so-and-so. His assistant will handle your query without you having to wait.' He easily outwitted the internal auditor to make us a modest profit on the postage account.

Nellie and Jim eventually became good friends, especially after my call-up to the RAF. On learning of the bestowal of wings he arranged an announcement in the *Leicester Mercury* with a photograph from which a sub-editor excised the large pipe to reveal my full face. Sensitive about the shape into which disability had forced his body, he was particular about his appearance and appreciated Nellie's allowing him discounts on the bespoke tailoring which she arranged. Love eventually bloomed via the switchboard with another telephonist into a happy marriage, and he and his wife became ardent supporters of Leicester Tigers, the rugby *wunderkinds* for whom the great Alexander Obolensky had played. I remember how badly Jim took the news of his death in a flying accident early in 1940, his Hurricane, as I later learned, having dropped into a ravine at the end of the runway during a training exercise at a Suffolk airfield.

Apart from directing callers to the right – and sometimes wrong – department, my job entailed: relieving Jim on the switchboard; dealing with the incoming and outgoing mail; delivering by hand local mail (a fertile field for flirting with female office workers); and running errands for the secretaries on the first floor (with whom a more or less flirtatious relationship was carried on). When, on the outbreak of war, Peggy married, the girls in Lucas E's outer office coached me for the ordeal of 'giving her away', which I performed with becoming seriousness, spoiling this at the reception by suggesting to her new husband that she must be worth at least a hundred Senior Service cigarettes.

After about a year with Jim I moved upstairs to the spacious office presided over by Mr Cyril Lancelot Launder, who chose to be known as Dick. He was effectively the chief clerk, and not a sparrow fell in Grey Friars without Dick's being aware of it. Under his benevolent tuition I began to learn the bureaucratic ropes, the backroom treadmill gradually giving way to more interesting duties involving direct contact with council members.

Pretty well all of those members would have passed Dick's Stinkers test as, until the post-war Labour landslide, the shire counties were no place for those of a socialist persuasion. I got the impression that if a stray trade unionist *had* succeeded in getting elected his only chance of an invitation to a pheasant shoot would have been as a beater. But as a junior I found most of them thoughtful and kindly, even if their speeches sometimes betrayed a marked abhorrence of bureaucracy. Fiery Major Guy Paget, for instance, in objecting on principle to any increase in staff, would always refer to them as *clerks*, even where the proposal was for teachers or surveyors rather than pen pushers. But he had written a readable book on Leicestershire in the *County History* series so I was saddened on learning soon after the war that he'd come a fatal cropper while out hunting – though glad to think he would probably have been carried from the field on one of the

Leicestershire five-barred gates (specially designed to be removable and used as a stretcher for hunting casualties).

One of my early jobs was manning the attendance register at quarterly meetings, ensuring that each arrival signed in. I particularly recall: bluff Sir Arthur (later Lord) Hazlerigg's invariable greeting of 'Mornin' young man'; the martial entry of Council Chairman Colonel Robert Martin (knighted after the war); and handsome, bearded Mr J T Jacques, long-term chairman of the Roads & Bridges Committee, who always put me in mind of a Radio Times illustration of Brahms. The diminutive Victor Pochin, re-elected year after year as vice to the Colonel, was always assiduous in enquiring about my progress, though one always had to remember to pronounce his name 'Puchin' to distinguish him from Mr 'Poachin', humble head of the motor vehicle taxation department.

I look back fondly at these Leicestershire worthies of seventy-odd years ago, many of which have been spent decrying Stinkers in the mass, though rarely as individuals.

Aside from my burgeoning administrative duties there was an odd arrangement whereby four times a year the Department switched from being concerned with meetings and other functions of a clerkly kind to servicing the ancient Court of Quarter Sessions, which in each county exercised a mainly criminal jurisdiction.

So, four times a year, Lucas E would don wig, gown and bands to transform himself into *Clerk of the Peace*, sitting in one of the ancient courtrooms of what remained of Leicester Castle in the Newark (*New Work* – naturally, one of the oldest parts of the City). There, his job was to read out the indictments and proffer legal advice to the Chairman of Sessions, a county bigwig who would be sitting on high with a panel of magistrates dispensing justice in those cases too serious to be tried at petty sessions (magistrates courts) but not grave enough to go to the Assizes. All was swept away in the post-war local government reforms, much to the regret of the Rumseys and their successors who so prized the ancient office that their national talking shop (and golf-playing sub-stratum) was called the *Clerks of the Peace*

Society, even though these court duties were but a miniscule part of their overall responsibilities.

I became one of the small team which would drop everything at Sessions time to make the short journey down Friar Lane to the court, pushing the Castle Chariot (a two-wheeled handcart used for transporting the relevant law books, files and sundries), which at first I felt self-conscious about in case a chance-met girl acquaintance might take me for a well-dressed plumber.

There, for some days, sometimes stretching to a week, we would establish our HQ in the indictment chamber next to the courtroom and make ourselves useful in various ways – seeing to the payment of witnesses' expenses, barristers' and solicitors' fees, and generally lurking about in a purposeful manner. We were on familiar terms with members of the local bar, several of whom were females whose allure was in most cases enhanced by a pertly perched wig.

In addition to the run-of-the-mill cases of larceny and dangerous driving we would occasionally be treated to misdemeanours of a more unusual kind, such as buggery (indecent relations with animals) – not all that unusual in country areas in the days before the pill-and-porn era. One always knew when such a case was about to come on as attendant police would begin slipping into the courtroom by side doors for what they would refer to as 'the dirt case', when those of us who were so minded would suddenly find it necessary to get a form signed or consult about a barrister's fee. After a particularly juicy case of this kind a larky colleague returned to the office from court shouting, 'Headline! Headline! Man insults pig!'

I was – and still am – particularly tickled by 'constable-speak' – the circumlocutions employed by police witnesses in court to describe unsavoury facts or behaviour. One I have never forgotten occurred in the case of a man up for wagging his willy at a woman in her village street, which the constable – 'refreshing his memory from a notebook' – described as follows (with face as straight as a yard of pump water): '*The complainant stated that the accused was exercising his person in a manner simulating self-abuse.*'

There would be ample time to explore what remained of the Castle – notably John O'Gaunt's Cellar with its collection of ancient weapons, and the muniment room with shelves of archives, including court rolls and the eighteenth century awards of land by the enclosure commissioners (which effectively marked the end of old England with its expanses of common land and vast fields of strip cultivation).

Mr Cashmore, a moustachioed ex-sergeant-major, was the Castle-Keeper, on the right side of whom it was important to keep. Fierce though he was, it took only a little wheedling to get his agreement to my liberating a few plants from the Castle Gardens for the apology of a rockery which I'd built behind Alf's garage.

Over the main entrance to the Castle Close was a splendid half-timbered house, rented to a private family until its conversion after the war to lodgings for His Majesty's Assize judges (who would be accommodated in great comfort with butler and clerk, between dealing with those delivered from the cells to stand trial, occasionally for their lives).

Before its adaptation judges were lodged in the County Rooms in Hotel Street, a fine eighteenth century building just down the road from the office, whose first floor was a magnificent ballroom with an Adam ceiling and other refinements in which the ghosts of Leicestershire's Jane Austens could be imagined dancing with scions of the Hazleriggs, Cromwells, Wartnabys and other county families. Just below the wide sweep of the stairs hung a fine painting of the ancient Melton Mowbray horse fair, and in a back room were faded photographs of yeomanry officers in pillbox caps.

The Council, not having a dedicated council chamber, held its quarterly meetings in the ballroom, although the acoustics were not good and much of what the aldermen and councillors said went unheard by those remote from the speakers.

Colonel (later Sir Robert) Martin, who chaired the Council for thirty-six years without a break, was a man of great clarity of diction who, when it was suggested that the chamber be wired for sound, opined that if members spoke up there would be no problem. He had a dry wit – on one occasion, when the sanitary arrangements at a particular school were being criticised, observing, 'Yerss – if they get much worse they'll be as bad as the school rears at Eton!' He could also enjoy a joke against himself – once, when visiting a county junior school, the fussy head, introducing him to a class, asked if anyone knew what he did. 'Yes, sir,' one piped up. 'He makes Bob Martin dog biscuits.'

During most wartime leaves I would call in to see Lucas E, Jim and such girls as were not on war service, noting that my progressive ranks had been posted on the entrance hall plaque of those serving in the armed forces.

Throughout the war my pension entitlements were preserved and, although I had doubts about a return to bureaucracy, marriage and paternity guided my post-war footsteps back to Grey Friars. After a reasonably successful career involving many moves I now enjoy an inflation-fattened pension, ring-fenced and about as safe from the predations of Chancellors of the Exchequer as Thornton reservoir was from the incursion of village children . . .

* * *

In September 2012, under the headline *Richard's skeleton reveals 'hunchback king'*, I was astonished to read that a team from Leicester University had unearthed in a city council car park a fully intact skeleton whose spinal abnormalities and head wound made it, as it were, a dead cert to be the remains of Richard III. They were long rumoured to have been laid to rest by friars in the church which occupied the site prior to 1538, when it was demolished during the dissolution of the monasteries. DNA tests later appeared to confirm that it was indeed so, and as I write arrangements are being made to have the remains re-buried in nearby Leicester Cathedral, although some claim that the city of York has a prior claim.

I quickly identified the site as the car park behind the Grey Friars headquarters of the County Council (which had moved some years after the war to a rather less stylish building beyond the city boundary). It therefore turns out that for some years before the war I had regularly walked to and from the cycle shelter over the royal remains, and post-war had parked my car, as near as I can judge, directly over the *locus in quo*.

I can't help wondering what my old mentor Jim would have made of the revelation had it come during his time at Grey Friars. I think that on the whole he would have been pleased that poor Richard was at last being accorded some respect after centuries of the cruel jibes which deformity has always provoked – including, no doubt, his own.

The Bennett 'Change'

On leave after my return from Canada, I was stepping out smartly towards the maiden aunts' boarding house in Leicester's Highfields district when I saw the pretty young daughter of one of the aunts' longer-term residents approaching. Instinctively, I snapped a salute before stopping to greet her. Years after the war she told me that it had been the thrill of her young life!

I suppose my tall slimness ('a long streak of piss' in the words of a drill corporal at Initial Training Wing in disparagement of my slow-march) did set off the RAF best blue to better advantage than on dumpier frames. In Leicester a splash of blue among the khaki was especially welcomed. The Royal Army Pay Corps was based in the city, hundreds of swaddies clumping through the streets in battledress and boots inviting remarks of the 'So when are you attacking the town hall?' variety.

Later in the war, after the aunts' long-term guests had all departed for the duration – and some for ever – their rooms were occupied by RAPC billetees, with in one case a happy outcome. But at present things were much as they had been during my childhood, when the comfortable three-storey house had been large enough to accommodate us at Christmas and in times of crisis.

How grudging those last words look on the page! There must have been many spinsters with room to spare whose hospitality was sparing, and the warmth of the maiden aunts' welcome was chalk to the refrigerated *Hillsborough* cheese, especially appreciated after the

Great Schism. Edith and Carrie were the aunts whom Bennett nieces and nephews saw most of, and the cake and biscuits which emerged from the corner pantry, a rarity at *Greyfell* during the lean years, were produced without undue delay as if they understood the agonies suffered by ravenous, sweet-toothed children faced with the insensitive priorities of most grown-ups.

Though not on a par with Galsworthy's *Change*, at Timothy's Bayswater house, where the extended Forsyte family would gather in time of crisis to seek reassurance from long-headed Soames, the house in St Peter's Road was where sooner or later you would meet all the Bennett aunts and uncles and their progeny. You would also, after Grandfather Bennett's death in 1925, have met Grandma Sarah, who lived with her daughters until her own time came in 1937.

Grandma Sarah with sister Peggy

Grandma was a kindly old lady, an undemonstrative Christian of the love-thy-neighbour variety, well able to quote from the family bible. Nellie often told us how, even during their poorest days in Thornton, her mother would make a pudding for anyone really up against it, popping it into the oven of the village bakery. She spoke fairly broad Leicestershire – a reproving, 'You mon't do that m'lad,' when I overstepped the mark, and a kindly, 'Never you mind ma duck,' if I suffered a disappointment. Somewhat troubled by constipation, she would express relief in words I still recall – 'I've moved me bowels this morning, Edie,' which, when I first heard them, gave me to wonder where she'd moved them to!

Life for women of her generation and class with large families and little money could be hard in a way now difficult to imagine, though Nellie's accounts of hard winters when her mother would be helping Robert to rescue sheep from snowdrifts brought it home to us. One epic had Sarah trudging miles in the snow when Robert was overdue from a trip to Leicester as 'common carrier' for Thornton and district, a sideline to boost his farming income. She found him exhausted, struggling to ascend an icebound hill near the city boundary. Between them they led the horse and wagon to the summit and ploughed on through the night, reaching home in the small hours.

She was the first dead person I saw and it was hard to connect the waxen mask with the kindly old lady who, like her youngest daughter, could entrance (and sometimes scare) you with her stories. This little song was hers, sung in a quavering voice:

> *Six o'clock is striking,*
> *Mother may I go out?*
> *My young man is waiting*
> *To take me round about.*
> *First he'll give me apples*
> *And then he'll give me pears*
> *And then he'll give me sixpence*
> *To kiss him on the stairs.*

I always felt that Edith should have married as she loved children. There was indeed a suggestion that, as with many women, the Great War's harvest of young men had spoiled her chances. Carrie didn't seem to be the marrying kind – but who knows what thwarted desires lurked behind her bird-like eyes?

To alleviate Nellie's lot during the years of struggle after Alf's departure Mildred lived with the aunts more or less permanently between the ages of three and sixteen, attending local schools and later a city secretarial college. This was a great joy to them and she was a favourite with the guests. If anything, the arrangement deepened the affection between Nellie and her younger daughter, who anyway spent most weekends at *Greyfell*. Mildred remembers:

Mum and I spent many happy hours in the cinema – 6p for her, 3p for me. She would buy a bag of wholemeal biscuits from Woolworths and we always stayed to see the film twice – it was a continuing performance in those days. Charles Boyer and Irene Dunn were top of our list. I also remember seeing an Al Jolson film, mopping my tears on the way out, it was so sad! Another memory – the radio on Sunday evenings before mum took me back to the aunts. It held us in thrall – Les Misérables and Henry Ainley taking the part of Soames in Galsworthy's Forsyte Saga were the favourites. We would then set off to the terminus where mum would put me on the bus, herself cycling to save the fare, meeting me at St Peter's Church near the aunts.

The dining and sitting rooms at the front of the house were virtually forbidden territory while guests were in residence, but open to exploration during their absence at Christmas and during the summer holidays when their books, wall-rack with many-shaped pipes, walking sticks, hat stand with its assortment of headgear (one I remember with 'Not Yours' on the inner band!) could be inspected. The pre-war boarders, mostly long-term, were nearly all businessmen based in Leicester but with homes elsewhere. A number were 'varsity' men whose high spirits led them into larks, some of which scandalised the aunts (though they enjoyed recounting them). Hanging a chamber pot on the arm of a nearby lamp-post is one I recall, and they were always teasing Carrie. During the 1945 general election campaign Peggy's husband John and I carried on this tradition by pasting Labour Party posters on the ground floor windows under cover of darkness. As the aunts had displayed Conservative posters in the upper windows there was puzzlement among the neighbours.

After the war Mildred married a handsome ex-RAF man who was boarding with the aunts — much to their delight. They had a second cause for celebration when Nance's elder daughter was carried off by one of the Royal Army Pay Corps soldiers billeted with them. Bert fooled the scoffers by becoming the combative Lord Mayor of his native city after the post-war Labour landslide.

Aunt Nance — she whom Nellie had teased as a child — lived with her five children in a terraced house not far from the aunts. Though perpetually harassed in her struggle to keep the crowded house in some sort of order, she was a typical Bennett in the warmth of her welcome, even if the edible hospitality never reached her sisters' standard.

There was no bathroom so the aunts made theirs available to Nance's teenage daughter — the future Lady Mayoress. It had a glass panel over the door and on one occasion when I was staying with them I climbed onto a chair and peeped through, intent on improving my scant knowledge of the female form divine. Disappointingly, I saw nothing through the steamy glass, but she must have twigged what I was up to as I received a stern lecture from Edith on the evils of Peeping Tomery.

Uncle Bob and aunt Ginnie, who had kept the pub where Grandpa had died but were now living in Leicester, were fairly frequent visitors. Ginnie was a pale, soft woman, approached with caution by nieces and nephews as her kiss suggested the embrace of a codfish. Her quavering presence gave no hint of the courage she showed in Bob's last illness during the bitter winter of 1946-7 when day after day she would make the trip to the General Hospital. I accompanied her on a couple of occasions, and queuing for the bus in the biting wind nearly finished me.

Bob's war had been spent in Mesopotamia – Mespot – generally considered to be cushier than the Western Front, though what it lacked in mud and machine guns it made up for in heat, dysentery and typhoid, the whole misconceived campaign being on a par with the Bush-Blair Iraq war (in which his unseen great nephew, Royal Marine son of my second marriage, took part).

Bob's elder brother, Harry, was tenant of the farm in quaintly named Hugglescote (where Phil and I had pitched our tent before the war). He was rarely to be seen at the aunts' after Grandma's death, but when he did visit there would be a chicken – or at harvest-time a rabbit (with lead shot embedded!) for Carrie to pluck or skin and prepare (now an almost forgotten domestic skill).

Florrie, the eldest aunt, lived with Uncle Jack Barnes in the small village of Stanton-under-Bardon in 'Bennett Country', Bardon being the granite-rich hill which a quarrying company was – and still is – reducing in the interests of highway improvement and house-driveway surfacing. The young Graham in pre-war days unwittingly did his best to boost the company's profits by bringing home pocketfuls of the product from a road repair heap on the main road, in a little-by-little attempt to enhance the thin layer of gravel which Alf had thought sufficient for *Greyfell's* driveway following the erection of the garage.

Their sons, Eric and Bert, worked for the quarry company and I have a memory of waving to them on the footplate of one of the narrow-gauge locomotives that hauled the stone to the crusher, which involved crossing the village street. We lads would place nails on the line in various patterns for the wheels to fuse. The giant crusher ground away at the bottom of a field and, during one of the troubled times at home when I was staying there, a play-fellow became too curious about the machinery, was drawn in and crushed. This disturbed my dreams for some time and I still think of him and those, including Eric and Bert, who had to retrieve the remains.

Looking back over half a century or more I salute the Bennett aunts and uncles for the sense of worth with which their kindness and hospitality endowed me – the awareness that in their eyes 'Nellie's boy' was, like his mother, a bit special.

A SEA CHANGE

Treading water

If the Manchester experience was frustrating, the months between returning from Canada to blackouts and rationing (and the achievement of operational status) were purgatorial.

First came the summons to an EFTS for a three-week course flying . . . *Tiger Moths*! On our questioning the need for this *entr'acte* we were told that the navigational skills of those returning from Canada were so poor that an intensive map-reading course was necessary before they were turned loose on valuable operational aircraft. It was difficult to disagree: if disorientated over the plains of Saskatchewan one had only to swoop down on the nearest grain elevator to read the name of the adjoining settlement – a variation of flying by the seat of one's pants.

After some pride-swallowing I found re-acquaintance with the friendly and forgiving little biplane quite enjoyable. Particularly pleasant was a joyride to Perth (the Scottish one!) with a friendly little Welsh P/O navigator, though I had to do most of the navigating as he was airsick for much of the journey.

A sad postscript to this episode was news from Canada that Sergeant Moyer, my first instructor, had been killed in a flying accident which had badly injured his pupil – who had taken over my girlfriend.

The next step should have been to an OTU, final step before apotheosis as a fighter pilot. Instead I found myself in a batch destined for a transit centre in Harrogate, presumably to await an OTU vacancy, though I wondered . . . For some time I'd been aware of signs of sclerosis in the aircrew supply lines – a consequence, I supposed, of the over-anticipation of losses by the Great Warriors now in authority, blooded as they had been in the slaughter-days of the Somme and air battles over the Western Front. Gaps for filling.

Accommodation was again in a requisitioned hotel, much bigger and swankier than the one in Torquay, but far less pleasant as there was nothing to do but join the hundreds on morning parade – when the names and destinations of those whose posting had come through were announced. The uncalled were then free for the day to explore the classical esplanades and gardens of the city, or take a bus to the more down-to-earth pleasures of Leeds.

It was in Leeds that I met Doreen, a ready cuddler who worked at the city's telephone exchange. We had some close encounters in the double seats which were a feature of her local flea-pit, and one passionate session on a park seat which ended abruptly with a policeman shining his torch on us, demanding, 'What do you think you're up to, young man?' I was reminded of this much later when a barrack room comedian joked about a similar encounter:

> **Policeman:** *Now then, 'oo d'you think you are – Rudolph bloody Valentino?*
> **Young man:** *No, I'm Ben f***ing Hur!*

The food in the sergeants mess can only be described as, well, a mess (such as would have been rejected with Yorkshire bluntness by the hotel's peacetime clientele), which quickly drove me to Leeds where I spent much of the savings I'd managed to put by from my pay on lunches or suppers at Jacomelli's restaurant, which I believe still exists. A friendly orderly room corporal warned that post-war I'd regret eating into my savings in this way, but to my future regret I ignored him.

As if sensing that my *dolce vita* lifestyle was becoming dangerously enjoyable, the powers-that-be at last included '938 Harrison' in a small batch of postings, not to an OTU, but to something called a GR School – which turned out to be a General Reconnaissance course in preparation for a posting to Coastal Command, the maritime arm of the RAF.

Coastal Command – the Cinderella service! Long hours stooging over grey-green ocean wastes hunting U-boats which, even if caught on the surface, would probably have slipped beneath the waves before one's depth charges – or green paint – could be deployed, the only bit of excitement dodging flak from Royal Navy gunners who were said to be as trigger-happy as they were poor at aircraft recognition. How the chair-borne warriors must have chuckled as they pricked that over-confident would-be fighter boy for so unglamorous a role.

It was a deathly blow from which it took me a long time to recover – if I ever have. To misquote Dr Johnson: '*Every man thinks meanly of himself for not having been a Spitfire pilot.*' Even now, on the edge of sleep, I find myself downing an ME109, or shooting up trains in my Typhoon after D-Day, a favourite sequence being based on a reported incident in which a bomb dropped at low level into the entrance of a tunnel after a train had entered was followed by another at the exit, which sealed it in.

I was desperate to get off the posting, if necessary by the service equivalent of strike action. Being by now thoroughly disenchanted with the RAF, I even toyed with the idea of making my way to China to join General Chenault's *Flying Tigers* – the sort of daft idea which had inspired me to learn Turkish. After calming down I sought an interview with someone in authority and quickly appeared before an aged Squadron Leader whose faded wings shaded a row of medal ribbons.

He listened with more sympathy than my wild plea to be taken off the posting deserved, but could hold out no hope of a cancellation, advising that if I tried to take my protest further I might end up in limbo. 'The RAF doesn't like you to step out of line and, although you might not think so, there's probably a good reason for switching you to Coastal. I know for a fact that the situation in the Atlantic is desperate. At least you'll still be flying. Look at me – tethered to an office desk. Pegasus knackered!'

This calmed me down. I took his advice and, in retrospect, came to see that he was right. The RAF was not kind to those who kicked against the pricks for whatever reason. I was to come across cases of aircrew who'd lost their nerve during operational flying and been stripped of rank and flying badges for LOMF – lack of moral fibre – and reduced to sweeping hangar floors. The same flinty response to human weakness which had led to the shooting of deserters in the Great War.

Pegasus knackered! A Dakota DC3 in Rangoon

Whilst packing for departure I looked down at the squads lined up in the courtyard below and spotted David, a contemporary at City Boys who'd followed me to Grey Friars with a job in the Health Department. I knew he'd trained as a navigator, and now here he was on his way to an OTU. I have always regretted not nipping down to wish him well as, some time afterwards, chatting to Jim in the enquiry office during a seven-day leave, his distraught father appeared with news that he was 'missing believed killed'. The school's top swimmer, his crawl was pure poetry, putting my head-jerky attempts to shame. Another name for the school's roll of honour and the memorial plaque in the County Rooms with its legend, *Dulce et Decorum Es pro Patria Mori*, now and forever linked with Wilfred Owen's poem about poison gas casualties.

I was sorry to be saying goodbye to Doreen, whose company had softened the Coastal blow and whose mother, a pleasant little body, had welcomed me to their small terraced house. Dad, though, had turned out to be a Great War bore, most of his experiences having been of the non-combatant kind with few or no trench hours. I'd hoped on my last visit for a final session with Doreen on the front room sofa, but by the time he'd taken the hint and shuffled off to bed there was no time if I was to catch the last service bus back to Harrogate. With his disappointed daughter's connivance I expressed our frustration by moving the pins on his *Daily Sketch* war map to place the Red Army within reach of Berlin – a clear case of foresight.

* * *

The GR Course turned out to be entirely ground-based, concentrating on navigation, naval strategy and submarine warfare. It was more like a school or college than a typical service unit, with only a smear of RAF 'bull'. Most of the instructors were ex-teachers or college lecturers, with a sprinkling of naval officers and the odd Coastal Command navigator. Discipline was relaxed, accommodation and food almost up to Canadian standards, and its location, on the edge of Bridgnorth, convenient for forays into the Shropshire countryside on the Raleigh sports which I'd brought back from leave.

It was difficult during an early English spring in such surroundings to sustain the mood of gloomy resentment into which the end of the fighter pilot dream had plunged me. All the same, my top tunic button remained undone, as if in mourning, until a fellow course member suggested that it might be time to give up being a fighter boy unless, he added, I proposed to undo a second button in the hope that it might influence the powers-that-be to post me to a twin-engine Beaufighter squadron.

I took the point and began to take an interest in the lectures. The mysteries of Mercator projections, astro fixes, bubble sextants, and other aspects of the art of dead-reckoning navigation were not really to my taste – too much maths, raising the ghost of Mr Carter and my humiliations in the classroom. But the lectures on naval strategy I found fascinating, even if they did seem more relevant to the oak bottoms of Trafalgar than to the steely realities across the Channel.

I remember finding the names of the various cloud formations quite poetical: cirrus, stratus, altostratus, nimbostratus, stratocumulus, cumulonimbus . . . They seemed to echo Polonius's pedantic categorisation of plays in Hamlet: 'tragedy, comedy, history, pastoral, pastoral-comical, historical-pastoral, tragical-historical . . .' Cumulonimbus was my favourite – skimming the cloud tops, their fluffy amplitudes would always suggest the pink sugar bums of the nymphs scattered through Dick's Royal Academy volumes in *Wrestavon*!

There was a reasonable amount of time off, and whenever the lecture programme permitted – and sometimes when it didn't – I would take off on the Raleigh for long rides through the Shropshire countryside. Much Wenlock, Cockshutford and Cleeton St Mary might have been titles from Houseman's *The Shropshire Lad*. The people I met in remote pubs were, for the most part, farmers or farmers' sons and daughters (who seemed to find a lone pilot dropping in on them a welcome variation in their bucolic existence).

I see from my log book that in the terminal exam I achieved a respectable 71.7%, which qualified me for the next stage – Oxford. Not the dreaming spires but the Airspeed Oxford, a twin-engine aircraft on which hordes of pilots and navigators destined for Bomber or Coastal Command received their operational training before joining a squadron.

All my flying so far had been on single-engine aircraft so it was necessary to undergo a conversion course to twins, and for this I was posted to an Advanced Flying Unit at South Cerney near Cirencester in Gloucestershire. From there I was immediately transferred to an auxiliary field at Little Rissington, some twelve miles up the Roman Road near Bourton-on-the-Water.

The Oxford was an inoffensive machine, prang-proof in RAF-speak, though I did my best near the course end. After the taut handling of the Harvard I found it sloppy, like driving a pair of mules after galloping a thoroughbred (not that I'd done either). I solo'd after about seven hours' instruction, and altogether put in over forty hours of circuits and bumps, navigational trips, and day and night exercises, plus a week's Beam Approach instruction at a God-forsaken airfield in Cheshire, by which time I was so dispirited that I fell into a couldn't-care-less attitude of mind.

To ease the tedium during solo night flights I took to annoying anti-aircraft searchlight crews who seemed to be training in the area, by flying moth-like into beam after beam, each one of which would be switched off as I entered. In this way time passed more agreeably, especially as the area was dotted with colour-coded navigational beacons called occults and pundits which, together with the on-off searchlights, made a *son et lumière* display against the darkened landscape. Whenever I've motored along the A429 *en route* to or from Stratford upon Avon or the Midlands I've recalled those dreamlike circlings above Bourton, Evesham, Stow-on-the-Wold and Moreton-in-Marsh.

This attitude resulted in a singular mishap which might well have got me slung off the course – or even grounded. Landing one day after a solo exercise, instead of operating the lever which raised the wing-flaps I absent-mindedly operated the adjacent toggle which retracted the undercarriage. To the hooting of the warning device the aircraft staggered to its knees like a sick camel, airscrews chewing the grass. In the petrified silence that followed I saw groundstaff running towards me and prepared for a showdown.

Fortunately, my flight commander, Flight Lieutenant Coke-Kerr, a pleasant South African with whom I got on well, was so surprised when I confessed to pulling the wrong lever instead of blaming the malfunctioning of the hydraulic system, that he defended me strongly when I was marched before the Commanding Officer on a charge of negligently damaging one of His Majesty's aircraft. I was let off with a period confined to camp and a red ink endorsement in my log book. The station's relaxed discipline made it easy to sneak out on the Raleigh through a side gate to enjoy sunny Cotswold excursions. The ink used for the endorsement must have been of wartime quality as it was expunged to unreadability when the relevant page was exposed to the weather.

After that narrow escape I pulled myself together and did Coke-Kerr fairly proud in the passing-out results. And that, on 9 July 1943 was effectively the end of my tortuous flying training programme – fifteen long months since I had taken off in Neepawa, Manitoba, aboard Tiger Moth No 1350 with gentle Sergeant Moyer. Quite a contrast with the minimal training received by pilots during the Great War and the desperate days of the Battle of Britain before being pitched into combat.

Crewing-up

The OTU was one step short of a squadron and indeed, in the much publicised thousand-bomber attack on Cologne of 30 May 1942, Bomber Command OTUs had been raided to make up the magic number. It was not the only time, though Air Chief Marshall Harris discontinued the practice when casualties became 'unacceptable'.

I was posted to 3 (Coastal) OTU and told to report to Cardington in Bedfordshire, one of the oldest RAF permanent stations. After ten days' leave I arrived there with a few others to find that it had just been moved to a coastal airfield near Haverfordwest in Pembrokeshire – which seemed a wise move as the sea had long since retreated from Bedfordshire. So off we went with fresh rail warrants, spending a few hours in London *en route*, gaping at the London Pride-infested bombsites – forever associated with Noël Coward – before catching our connection at Paddington.

After the usual stop-start journey the first view of the Haverfordwest airfield from the train was uninspiring – a clutch of grey administrative buildings surrounded by wooden and Nissen living quarters, control tower, ops block, petrol bowsers and wind sock . . . indistinguishable from the many other UK airfields I was to serve on or visit over the next two years.

Scattered round the field were about a dozen shabby Wellingtons in once-white Coastal livery, each with a row of aerials sprouting from its back, soon to be identified as part of the early Air-to-Surface-Vessel system (ASV – better known as radar) invented by the boffins as an aid to detecting ships and surfaced U-boats at night or in conditions of poor visibility. With the squat undercarriage and portly fuselage, these suggested a pregnant duck crossed with a stickleback, and immediately plunged me into a slough of Bedfordshire Bunyan's despond at the contrast with the classic lines of a Spitfire or Hurricane. If anyone had predicted that I would come to have a wry affection and respect for the Wellington I would have, as my friend Ronald might have put it, micturated myself laughing.

Between 29 July and 24 August 1943 the crew I had joined was detailed to carry out four operational flying exercises (a Coastal version of the Bomber Command *milk runs*, low-risk introductions to an operational tour) – these besides bombing exercises, air firing and fighter affiliation. They were basically 'dead reckoning' navigation exercises, each lasting about a couple of hours. The object of one was to find Rockall, an isolated outcrop in the Atlantic, inevitably dubbed F***all by those who failed to find it. We did, but otherwise our trips went far from smoothly due to bad weather and engine or equipment trouble – the chief curses of Coastal Command and much other long-distance flying during the war.

It was the special difficulty of completing the fourth exercise that led Stanley and I to show off our school French by adopting *Faites OFE 4 Encore!* as the crew motto. Stanley has already been mentioned as the crew member seeking solace among the swirling frills of Carmen Miranda's dress after we'd flown within sight of the lights of Coruna. A Liverpudlian, handsome in a Nordic way, he had, like a number of Dunkirk veterans, exchanged khaki for blue, appalled at the apparent lack of allied air cover during the evacuation.

The second and third Wop/Ags were Ron and Rex. The former, a tall Londoner with the practical skills of a boy scout, had the curious habit of suddenly disappearing if you were out walking with him. Rex, the youngest and shortest of the three, with a compensatory pencil moustache, was best suited to the cramped rear gun turret, though the custom was for the three to man wireless, radar and guns turn and turn about.

Bob (the Canadian navigator) had been a dentist. Though cheerful on the ground he was apt to be short-tempered aloft when his face would screw itself into the semblance of a shelled walnut. The navigator was usually the most hard-worked member of a Coastal Command crew, constantly irritated at being told he'd lost the plot.

Our Flight Lieutenant captain, Alan, had been a pre-war member of the RAF's Volunteer Reserve, aerial equivalent of the Territorial Army. Mobilised at the outbreak, he had (as already mentioned) done a tour of operations on Beauforts followed by a 'rest'. Now here he was, faced with a second tour of four hundred hours or so of mostly night flying with a rooky crew.

As a Victorian novelist might have put it, he was of middle height, light of build with a springy step. Quite handsome in a refined sort of way, an opinion obviously shared by the smiling woman on the dressing table in his quarters, he was proud of their recently born twins, though recalling that the celebratory shoot-up at nought feet by squadron colleagues had put the wind up their mother. In the way he wore his service cap – dead straight, peak shading his eyes – he reminded me of those faded photographs of Great War naval pilots standing by their stringbag flying machines.

It took him a while to get used to the Wellington, which must have been heavier to handle than the Beaufort. Initially he was tending to 'land' ten feet off the ground in what Bob growlingly called a Waygood Otis (elevator) effort. The RAF seemed to enjoy assigning not-so-tall pilots to multi-engine aircraft while confining gangling fellows such as Roald Dahl in the cramped cockpit of a Spitfire or Hurricane. But Alan soon mastered the aircraft and became a first-rate Wimpy pilot, promoted to Squadron Leader at the end of his second tour – and the war.

There was little time to explore the area surrounding the airfield, though we did manage several trips to the nearby coast, where the swimming was good. Years after the war, a biography of Augustus John informed me that he was born in the small town of

Haverfordwest, a few miles south of the airfield, and as a young man had cracked his head diving from the rocks near where we'd swum, after which, the tale went, he changed from a fairly quiet type to the bearded extrovert of the painting years. Perhaps if history had repeated itself I might have taken a less supine attitude to the machinations of the thick rings and barged my way Bader-like into a fighter cockpit!

After thirty-seven hours flying as a crew we were passed fit for operations and learned that after seven days' leave we were to join 612, a Coastal Command squadron based at Chivenor in North Devon – Glorious Devon, familiar to me from Peter Dawson's rich baritone voice rolling out of the twisty-legged gramophone, but otherwise *terra incognito*.

It was now that the advantage of being crewed with a senior officer of some experience became apparent. On past postings, details of what to expect on arrival had remained a mystery until – arrival. Now, Alan was able through the unit's adjutant – with whom he'd served previously – to obtain fairly full information about the squadron.

612 Squadron

Formed at Dyce near Aberdeen in 1937, its full title was *612 (County of Aberdeen) Squadron, Auxiliary Air Force* with the motto *Vigilando Custodimus (We Stand Guard by Vigilance)*, though Bob, who never took to the watery wartime sauce – or to English wartime food generally – translated it as *Beware of the Goddam Custard*.

The squadron's early guard-standing abilities must have been severely circumscribed by a succession of inadequate aircraft, commencing with the Avro Anson, a twin-engine reconnaissance machine soon to suffer the indignity of yellow livery as a training aircraft, but serving with 612 until November 1941 when conversion to the longer-range Armstrong Whitworth Whitley was completed. The squadron endured this slab-sided aircraft with its in-line engines prone to glycol leaks until June 1943 when conversion to the first maritime version of the Wellington was completed.

612 Squadron badge

After Dyce, there were spells at Wick in the extreme north-eastern highlands, Reykjavik in Iceland (brrr!) and Thorney Island in Hampshire. Then came the big change when the squadron became one of the first to be fitted with the Leigh Light and moved to Devon, settling in May 1943 at Chivenor, an airfield bordering the estuary of the Tawe east of Barnstaple, part of 19 Group, Coastal Command.

Wellington with Leigh Light lowered

Still there, the airfield has over the years accommodated all kinds of RAF and Fleet Air Arm units. Long having intended to revisit it, my wife and I finally made it in the autumn of 2011 during a short Devonshire holiday.

Nothing was as I'd remembered it. The guardroom, which once scowled over the entrance gates, had been replaced with what looked like a well-designed toilet block, and the cool appraisals of the corporals replaced by a pleasant smile on the face which appeared at the enquiry window. Without fuss I was handed a pass to what I understood to be the only remaining RAF unit – 21 Squadron RAF, an Air-Sea Rescue outfit sharing the field with Royal Marines and others.

612 Wimpy being towed by a WAAF at Chivenor, April 1944

As we drove slowly along the main thoroughfare 'others' appeared to be industrial units of one kind or another, and indeed, the whole site seemed to resemble a larger version of the 'industrial estate' one comes across on remote greenfield sites throughout the Kingdom, lured there by government grants (and these days usually replete with 'units to let' signs).

My monochrome memories of parachute store, ops block, hangars, control tower, runways, perimeter track, aircraft at dispersal and the clusters of living quarters were progressively expunged and the Air-Sea Rescue unit (when we finally reached it) seemed to be begging for rescue from the encroaching concrete. There was no chance of a lap of honour round the perimeter track for a veteran Coastal pilot!

A Chinook helicopter lay at rest outside the squadron HQ and, after a tour of the operations room, a friendly crew member showed me over it – my first introduction to a military helicopter. Underawed by its size and the complexity of cockpit and controls, I came away reinforced in my preference for wings – even the Wimpy's flapping ones – over a horizontal windmill.

* * *

This profile of the squadron turned out to be incomplete as I discovered when, after the marriage of my second son David, I found that his wife Valerie was something of an expert on the history of wartime flying, with a special interest in Bomber Command. That she had also researched a more lightweight aspect of the war in the air became clear when a cardboard box was produced containing information on a little-known aspect of the war – when 612 had been given a key role in the reaction of the powers-that-be to the threat of an opening attack by German naval forces.

'*When the balloon went up*' was a phrase much in use for the day war broke out, but '*When the moths fluttered off*' might have been more apt as 612 was one of about half a dozen squadrons round the Kingdom's perimeter chosen to form coastal patrol flights of unarmed, open-cockpit Tiger Moths – the DH82s I'd done initial training on – charged with spotting and reporting the position of quick-off-the-mark enemy naval vessels. Christened *Scarecrow*

Patrols, their pilots were probably more scared than the crows as they weighed the chances of survival should engine failure or other emergency force them into the icy North Sea, the only heating system being a hot-water bottle.

No enemy ship, sub or surface, is known to have been encountered, a precedent which we and most other Coastal Command crews were to follow throughout the war, the shivering pilots doubtless consoling themselves with Hamlet's philosophical: *The readiness is all.* The Tiger Moth flight and others round the coast were stood down as soon as the more operationally adequate aircraft had taken over.

* * *

On my ninetieth birthday I became aware of a mythical aspect of 612 when Fabrice, my youngest daughter's partner, presented me with an English translation of Antoine de Saint-Exupéry's *Le Petit Prince*, which I'd never got round to reading (though an admirer of his *Pilote de Guerre* and *Courier Sud*). In the opening chapter about the Prince's planetary origins I read: *I have good reason to believe that the Prince's planet was B.612.*

Having been saddened by St Ex's end-of-war disappearance on a reconnaissance trip piloting an American Lockheed Lightning – the one with cockpit capsule oddly isolated between twin booms – I could now star him in a fantasy flight over Biscay to join his *destined* squadron, entrusting himself to the less glamorous, but more friendly, Wimpy with every prospect of enjoying, as I have, a ripe old age.

Operations

I arrived at the airfield in September 1943 after what is remembered as a muted seven days' leave, trying to make the posting sound less unglamorous than it was. As the train snaked along the airfield boundary it was a relief to see that the aircraft at dispersal were smarter looking than the OTU pregnant sticklebacks. Although nothing could have been done about the ducks' disease, dorsal smoothness had been achieved at the cost of a prominent chin under the perspex bay window – a faint suggestion of Uncle Sam's wispy beard. This was soon revealed as the rotating scanner of the boffins' latest magic box, the Mk III centimetric radar – a map-based invention which painted on the operator's screen a phosphorescent image of the land or seascape over which the aircraft was passing (and perchance a surfaced U-boat).

In the far corner of the airfield, as if trying to dissociate themselves from the porky Wimpys, was a flight of photographic reconnaissance unit (PRU) Spitfires in their sky-blue livery, the sight of which plunged me into a deeper shade of blue.

I found the three Wop/Ags installed in the sergeants mess. Ron soon did his disappearing trick while the other two led the way to the comfortable billet they'd secured at the end of one of Mr Nissen's tunnel-shaped hutments, complete with coal-burning stove and surprisingly comfortable beds. On rejoining us, Ron trotted out the information he'd been able to gather, most of which turned out to be 'pukka gen' (boghouse rumours were 'duff gen').

The aircraft were Mk XIVs, replacing the OTU Mk XIIs, the main improvement (apart from the radar) being the replacement of the Bristol Pegasus engines with the more powerful Hercules. Two other Leigh Light Wimpy squadrons shared the airfield – 304 and 407, respectively Polish and Canadian.

We met Alan in the operations block and were soon joined by Bob, whose bleary-eyed appearance, we later learned, was due to the excesses of a leave spent in London's Strand Palace Hotel – notorious during the war for orgiastic behaviour – after which he had, in his own words, 'gone up with the blinds'. So here we all were, operational at last.

We four NCOs were in the mess the evening after the second ops trip described earlier, celebrating our new status by joining with a couple of other crews in the beery rendering of a Bomber Command peon to the Wellington, to the tune of *Waltzing Matilda*, unaware as yet of the fate which had overtaken the crew patrolling the 'box' next to ours:

> *Ops in a Wimpy, Ops in a Wimpy*
> *Who'll come on ops in a Wimpy with me?*

Swinging into the now forgotten remainder of the refrain, we were joined at the bar by two Warrant Officer Wop/Ags in blue tunics best described as 'commissioned officer manqué', and of a well-worn appearance indicating much seniority – which was emphasised by their joining in the chorus substituting 'Whitley' for 'Wimpy', a politer way of saying, 'Get some in' (meaning operational flying hours).

We were then launched into another chorus, this time to the well-known army tune of *Bless 'em all*, which seemed tailor-made for the Chivenor squadrons, and as the beer flowed the seeming promise of an action-packed tour restored some of my enthusiasm for flying, though perhaps Stanley and Ron, both married, were less keen (they need not have feared!):

> *A Wimpy was leaving the Bay*
> *Bound for old Blighty's shore,*
> *Heavily laden with terrified men,*
> *Shit-scared and prone on the floor.*
> *There's many a Heinkel been pumping its lead,*
> *And many a Messerschmitt too:*
> *They've shot off our bollicks*
> *And f***ed our hydraulics,*
> *So cheer up my lads, bless 'em all.*

We got to know the two W/Os well during the following weeks of training between operational trips. Their reminiscences of hazardous flights 'up the Skaggerat' and patrolling off Greenland with ice forming on the Whitley's wings, often staggering back to base nursing an engine leaking glycol, made me appreciate our more shapely and reliable aircraft with its Bristol radial engines personifying power as they roared away on the gently vibrating wings.

We learned that instead of being posted away for the usual rest after completing their tour on the squadron, they had been retained as instructors on the new radar and an improved wireless.

Although the full significance of 'centimetric' was beyond my unscientific mind, their assurance that it was way ahead of anything the Germans possessed was encouraging. What I couldn't understand as the tally of our operational sorties mounted was why, during the long hours patrolling the Bay, the magic screen with its slowly rotating strobe had so far failed to identify on the boundless ocean anything that looked like a submarine.

There had been, during our fourth trip, a contact in the Bay west of St Nazaire which Ron as our radar whiz-man thought might be worth investigating. Although it appeared not to be moving it just might be a surfaced U-boat in some sort of trouble, to which we might usefully add. So, after circling round the area for a while Alan decided to investigate.

A Leigh Light attack had to follow a strict pattern, requiring much practice. On picking up the radar contact the operator would home the pilot onto it, height being adjusted to 250 feet as indicated on the radio altimeter – more accurate than the pressure-based one. Meanwhile, the second dicky would move forward to the nose, lie flat on the bench and prepare to direct the beam onto the target by means of a short control column, with one of the Wop/Ags coming from the rear to stand astride him ready to direct fire from the nose machine guns onto whatever revealed itself. At about six miles from the contact the light would be lowered hydraulically, and at one mile switched on and the beam raised until it illuminated the target.

On this occasion all it revealed was an elongated French Rockall, and although this was disappointing, had it been the real thing we might have shared the fate of those who'd made the attack off the Spanish coast. The outcome was frustrating, but at least more fun than the usual Leigh Light drill involving a Royal Navy vessel, even if our ex-allies on the sleeping mainland might have trotted out the dismissive remark of Maréchal Bosquet on hearing of the Charge of the Life Brigade: '*C'est magnifique, mais ce n'est pas la guerre*' (or perhaps more accurately, '*Ce n'est pas magnifique, mais c'est la guerre!*').

Under the expert tuition of our instructors, Ron soon learned to distinguish these rock contacts from the real thing ('When we've finished with you you'll be able to tell whether a *matelot* peeing over the side is Jew or gentile!').

A successful attack by a Canadian crew of 407 Squadron soon after our arrival lifted our spirits a little, but there was no repeat until a month later an attack by a 612 aircraft was confirmed as a kill. I remember W/O Gunn, the skipper, as a quiet man, not given to bar-propping and a stickler for crew training – the best sort of Coastal pilot. The only time I saw him at all excited was when he and his crew entered the ops block for de-briefing after the successful operation.

Confirmation of a kill often had to await the war's end and examination of German naval records as a U-boat would often have partially or wholly submerged by the time an attack was pressed home, and if there was no evidence of a hit (such as surface wreckage or a substantial oil slick) there was always the possibility that it had survived.

Disenchantment set in as 1943 slipped into 1944 with much appalling weather and nothing to show in my log book but 'A/S Patrol' or similar, quite often supplemented by 'R/B (Return to Base) engine trouble', 'Diverted to . . . (fog at Base)' or, more frequently, 'Recalled weather'. I've just totted up – for the first time – the number of operational flights aborted for one reason or another throughout my tour of operations. The total comes to eleven out of the forty-nine flown.

It was a mystery to us – and to other crews I'm sure – why the magic new radar was not revealing more targets for the eight 250 lb depth charges (two sticks of four) in our bomb bays which, with the heavy Leigh Light gear and 800 gallons of high octane fuel, made prising the aircraft from the runway on take-off so physically wearing.

We knew there had been a glory period following the first deployment of the Leigh Light in 1942, though it was a sister squadron, 172, which had been the first to use it in anger, enjoying a *success de surprise* that was still reverberating round the mess when I joined 172 with my own crew in November 1944. We were also aware that there had been so great a slaughter among Grand Admiral Doenitz's mid-Atlantic 'wolf packs' earlier in 1943 that convoys were now passing through virtually unscathed.

As usual, the security blanket muffled details, but the Coastal Command grapevine had now and then broken through with rumours of great success by the Liberators and Sunderlands circling the convoys, including a double kill on the same day by an ace sub-hunter. Such riches!

Meanwhile, we were left to burrow through the darkening winter clouds, with the hungry waves of the 'Bay of Whisky' all too near below. U-boats proceeding to or from their heavily fortified bases on the French coast still had to pass through the Bay and there was some consolation in assurances by those in authority – and our own awareness – that we were making life miserable for the U-boaters, who could scarcely put their conning towers above the surface either by night or by day without being spotted either visually or by radar. This meant more hours breathing the foul interior air – and slow progress – as underwater speed running on batteries instead of diesels was much reduced.

The story of this final phase in the U-boat war is a fascinating one, much of it hidden from the eyes – even of those who took part in it – by a security blanket thicker than Atlantic fog, which took years to clear. Separating my own recollections from the many post-war publications on all aspects of the anti-submarine war would be impossible, so with the recent commemorative events celebrating the seventieth anniversary of 'Victory in the Atlantic', I have thought it appropriate to add a brief account as background to this memoir (see page 150).

The battle has turned – a U-boat being attacked on 8 October 1943

And another on 5 November 1943 – notice the cowering crew

Stations of the Cross

Sometimes, it seemed that the time spent in the air was the least significant part of an operation. It was the long-drawn-out preliminaries which consumed our energy, tried our patience and left us roaring down the runway with a mixture of exhaustion and relief at being airborne at last.

Each operation was preceded by a flight-test of up to an hour so that captain and crew could satisfy themselves that the aircraft and equipment were in good order. The day had long gone when each crew was assigned its own aircraft whose every characteristic would be as familiar as those of a wife or mistress. Wartime expansion had brought in the O & M experts – who devised a system called *planned maintenance*, the aeronautical equivalent of wife-swapping.

Unfortunately, some aircraft resented being made to work harder and tended to go on strike. On our early trips S-Sugar was a particularly black sheep in white camouflage, and whenever drawn in the operational lottery particular care was taken during the test to run a strict ruler over her. One or other of Sugar's engines had the habit of developing a weakness half-way through a trip, which the hydraulics system or radio sometimes found to be contagious. Eventually, Sugar went into a decline, like a woman rejected after serial unsuccessful face-lifts, and was replaced.

Ex abundante cautela, as we lawyers like to say, a wise captain would also do a quick personal inspection of the aircraft immediately before take-off to ensure that ailerons, elevators and other moving surfaces moved, and that the protective cover over the small tube invented by a M. Pitot, through which airspeed was measured, had been removed.

Alan was assiduous in carrying out these last-minute checks and I remember an occasion early in our journey together when his sharp eye spotted what appeared to be an oil leak from the area of the tail wheel. He summoned Chiefy, the senior groundstaff NCO who, after inspecting it, burst out laughing: 'I think a dog's peed on the wheel, sir.' The joke was that it had been Rex, a fellow Wop/Ag, having kidded him that it would bring luck and a measure of protection to the rear gunner! My own concession to superstition was Pinocchio, a soft-toy mascot made by my girlfriend and future wife, sometimes left behind with no ill consequences.

The pre-flight routine became especially wearisome as time went on. After the air test would come the briefing, which in our case bore no relation to the high drama of those post-war films in which a screen is pulled aside by the Richard Todd/Michael Redgrave type to reveal the 'target for tonight', bringing forth an audible gasp from the onlookers. In the Chivenor ops room there was only a large, unchanging chart of the Bay with the countries peripheral to it, every inch of the ocean laced with rhomboidal patterns of white tape indicating the patrol routes which the operational crews were to fly that night.

Almost always among the tape patterns there would be several fish-shaped symbols, each representing the estimated or last-reported position of a U-boat, and now and again we were lucky enough to observe the actual posting of a symbol on the chart by one of ops-room girls. Though the generality of WAAFs inspired few lustful thoughts in me – perhaps it was the flat shoes, lyle stockings and brass-buttoned tunic or shapeless battledress – it was generally agreed that the ops room girls were a cut above the average, and I confess to having on occasions stumbled into the outer darkness after a briefing with the fading image of a well-filled tunic and thighs taut in the placing of a symbol on the chart.

There was, I often thought, an element of sadism in the way the RAF ensured that those about to yield to night's cold embrace would be reminded of the warmer felicities which might be enjoyed during the unguarded small hours in the overheated atmosphere of the ops block. I was reminded of this on first reading Joseph Heller's *Catch 22* (and later seeing the film), where those being briefed for a suicidal mission break out in audible lust as General Dreedle's 'secretary' flaunts her charms ('*Ooooooooooooooh*,' *Yossarian moaned* . . .).

The years have expunged all but the vaguest memories of those who harangued us during the briefing process, with the exception of the meteorological officer, or metman, a carrot-topped little Scotsman whose predictions, delivered with a curious turn of phrase, have kept his image sharp, probably because the weather was our chief enemy.

'I'm going in for westerly winds of fifteen to twenty miles an hour and eight-tenths cloud at two thousand feet over most of the search area,' he might announce, 'but here over base it will be clear for take-off.' We often wondered why, before ending on this optimistic note, the chap hadn't thought to stick his head out of the ops block when he would sometimes have observed that, in the flying man's vernacular, it was 'ten-tenths and pissing down' with little sign of an early let-up. The balance of opinion among aircrew was that this would have been regarded by the met fraternity as cheating, like a member of the magic circle explaining a card trick.

Before a night operation we were advised to take a rest – preferably in the straight-and-level position – which, like children ordered to bed before a late-night pantomime, we usually did, though as with children sleep could rarely be bidden, and anyway, Chivenor was no more tranquil than other RAF stations.

Soon after arriving on the station I'd acquired a second-hand portable gramophone of the wind-up variety and a small collection of records discovered at the bottom of a pile in the mess, unloved and unplayed beneath the pop music of the day. The ones I remember are Elisabeth Schumann singing Brahms, Chopin preludes, Scarlatti harpsichord sonatas and Grieg's Peer Gynt suite. It became a ritual before an ops trip for the three Wop/Ags and myself to dance round the billet in our long-john aircrew underwear to the finale of the Grieg – *In the Hall of the Mountain King* – starting slowly and accelerating wildly to the music until the final crash. I like to think that my companions of the night were reminded of these Bachanalian-type scenes whenever in the years to come they chanced to hear the music.

Like many RAF stations Chivenor had a music club, and on one occasion I took the records, newly bought on leave, of William Walton's first (and then only) symphony, much of which was regarded as cacophonous. There was a shocked silence after the final crashing bars, but a WAAF officer came up to me afterwards and said that listening to it had helped resolve a troubling personal problem.

En route to the ops canteen for our pre-take-off meal of bacon and eggs, Fred the message carrier pigeon would be collected in his orange metal container – and signed for! Rex, whose Somerset uncle had been a pigeon fancier, usually undertook this task, cooing sympathetically into the tiny prison. Dear Rex was so easy to tease – Stanley and I would discuss using Fred for live bait to supplement the emergency rations should we have to take to the dinghy on ditching. Later, pigeons were phased out – not through pressure from the RSPCA, but because new navigational aids had made them redundant.

Each of us also collected an emergency pack which, besides such items as compass, map of the continent and other escape aids, contained glucose sweets and a tablet form of Horlicks malted milk, which pre-war advertising had recommended for those suffering from what they called 'night-starvation' (though *'Horlicks makes big Ballicks'* was the unofficial slogan). Other tablets, instead of encouraging sleep, were a form of drug known as *Wakey Wakey pills*, intended to keep the spirits up in a dinghy but sometimes used for 'recreational purposes' by forerunners of the drugs generation.

After the meal it was by transport to the crew room, a bare hut disfigured by peeling posters of the *Beware of the Hun in the Sun* variety and lined with lockers for our flying kit. On a few of the doors the faint chalk image of a U-boat recalled the brief killing season following the introduction of the Leigh Light, while bolder depictions of sailing boats recorded more recent attacks on Spanish fishing vessels or 'Seine netters' suspected of transmitting warnings of approaching aircraft to the enemy. *Attack anything that moves on the surface* was the writ running in the Bay.

Then out to the aircraft at dispersal, pausing *en route* for Alan to 'sign for the kite' as being fit to fly (Form 500 was it? I used to wonder if the captain of a battleship had to do likewise before leaving port), boarding, stowing parachutes and kit, and starting the engines on their long night's work before waving chocks away and crabbing to the runway end where Alan and I would go through the final checks before take-off (I still remember the mnemonic T M P F F, whatever it stood for!). The green 'clear for take-off' flash and then off, off into the dusk or dark.

At each one of these wearying stations of the cross I was haunted by newsreel images of Battle of Britain fighter pilots running to their aircraft, leaping into the cockpit and taking off like a graceful gaggle of geese towards the sun. Free as the air . . .

Dinghy, dinghy . . .

What can one say about those long winter patrols, more often than not in weather one wouldn't have wished on a dogfish? A scrotem-tightening occasion occurred in mid-Bay early in the tour when a Herculean coughing fit sent the needle on the starboard oil pressure gauge – normally as fixed as the dial on a child's pedal car – plunging wildly, gave a sour taste of what to expect. Activation of the fuel pressure balance cock restored things somewhat, but it was enough to send us back early. Fully laden, a Wimpy was not a good bet on one engine.

A close-up view of a naked Hercules under maintenance in the hangar always made me nervous. How could all that gadgetry keep working for hours on end without something coming loose and buggering up the works? I still feel the same about cars, and tend to lift the bonnet only when the screen-washer water has run out.

In any kind of emergency, height is the pilot's best friend. As our operations were normally flown at between 500 and 2000 feet above the waves one felt permanently friendless, rarely able, except on the smoothest of nights, to relax for long at the controls by switching in George, the automatic pilot. In the small hours, having lulled one to a comatose state, he would often slyly slip into a shallow descent, compounding the felony by straying from Bob's straight and narrow, prompting an injured, 'How about trying *my* course now?' over the intercom.

In between ops trips there would be Leigh Light training, gunnery practice with fighter affiliation, wireless and radar training for the

Wop/Ags, blind flying practice on the Link Trainer for Alan and I, genning up on aircraft and ship recognition, keeping up with intelligence reports, dinghy drill . . .

Dinghy drill! Practising on dry land the correct procedure for ditching and vacating a damaged or fuel-expired aircraft was (for obvious reasons) taken seriously in Coastal Command. Talismanic as the Mae West inflatable life jacket may have been as a life-saver, and reassuring as it was for each crew member to have a personal dinghy, it was the crew-size dinghy in the Wimpy's starboard wing which inflated on impact with the sea that gave the only real chance of survival in mid-ocean. The whistle worn on the battledress blouse of operational aircrew (as an aid to location of those floundering in the waves) completed the life-saving equipment, and was also valued as an accompaniment to rude songs on bibulous mess nights.

The realistic chance of surviving a ditching in the Bay – particularly at night – must have been slight. I can do no better than quote from *No Place to Land,* * a very readable book by a pilot of 304 Polish Squadron serving alongside us at Chivenor during roughly the same period:

> *We had . . . inexplicable losses of aircraft which disappeared without a trace. Flying at 500 feet during the night in all weathers was probably enough to account for most of the aircraft, and enemy action the others . . . While looking through air intelligence monthly reports I came across statistics on air/sea rescue operations. After the type by type breakdown of the aircraft involved, one element was all too clear. There were no rescues from the Wellington Mark XIV at all. Coincidence? I checked through more data. In total I found only two cases where the crews were saved . . . both rescues were carried out in shallow water fairly near the coast. What had happened to the others?*
>
> *My guesses focused on the recent modifications made on the Mark XIV: the front turret had been replaced by a perspex nose, and a retractable turret had been built into the fuselage for the Leigh Light.*

---

* *No Place to Land. J.F. Jaworzyn William Kimber Publishers*

In ditching, the nose would break under the pressure of the water, while the severe stress of hitting the sea would almost certainly break the fuselage in two. The nose, with the heavy engines, would go down at once, taking the dinghy with it; the tail section could not float by itself.

I came across the book some years ago in the small but fascinating Wellington Aviation Museum at Moreton-in-Marsh in Gloucestershire, whose proprietor, Gerry Tyack, had opened it as a sort of dedication to those who had trained during the war at Moreton airfield on bomber-version Wimpys. On display was a fascinating collection of artefacts and books relating to the Wellington, and Gerry couldn't have been more pleased when he learned that I was an ex-Wimpy pilot. The book, which he winkled out from a tight-packed shelf, had been published some years previously, and a number of pages in the middle had been muddled in the printing, which probably accounted for its having been remaindered with the opening pages (including details of the publisher) removed, so that although I made an effort to get in touch with the author I failed (lack of match-box lorry persistence?). Gracing the cover is an excellent action painting of a 304 Wimpy sweeping in low, bomb doors open, depth charges churning the sea.

612's dinghy drill took place on a retired, engine-less Wimpy in a hangar where crews could simulate the whole procedure, from the captain's command, 'Dinghy, dinghy, prepare to ditch!' to the taking up of safety positions before the final scramble through escape hatches onto the starboard wing. It was all a bit of a lark, though I well remember how taut Alan's body was as I helped him through the cockpit hatch, a measure of the strain he was under after years of operational flying.

The voluptuous dreaming which I indulged in during long night flights had a curious echo one evening in the early summer of 1944 when I entered the vast hangar intent on honing my moribund piloting skills with half an hour of blindfold cockpit drill. The dirty-white aircraft crouching abandoned in its corner, empty nacelles like sightless eyes, was a beached whale, its tall dorsal fin the only reminder of better days. As I paused in sad contemplation, a pair of trousered legs emerged from the entrance hatch, feet fumbling the ladder. I dodged behind a large crate, unobserved, and when the rest of the body appeared, recognised a corporal barman in the sergeants mess.

At the foot of the ladder he stood peering upwards as wrinkled blue-grey lisle stockings appeared through the hatch, with flat shoes seeking a rung, followed by the remainder of Clarice, a comely cookhouse WAAF.

I emerged as the couple disappeared arm-in-arm through a side door. On entering the fuselage there was evidence of a cosy nest behind the main wing spar: two carelessly folded blankets with a deflated 'air bed' to provide pneumatic relief from the chill metal floor. Clearly this had been a repeat assignation, understandable in view of the frustrating lack of privacy on the station.

So I wasn't the only one to have discovered that Barnes Wallis's geodetic fuselage could become a tunnel of loving dreams – and deeds!! Aroused by the vision of what had probably taken place behind the main spar I abandoned the cockpit drill.

* * *

There was very little contact with either the Polish or Canadians sharing the airfield with us. A squadron was very much an entity – a sort of closed shop – and anyway, there was in my recollection a tendency towards xenophobia among British servicemen as the number of those rallying to the cause from abroad increased, diluting the native effort.

American airmen operating over here were generally regarded as Johnny-come-latelies, inclined to make a drama out of what the RAF had been doing without a lot of fuss since the outbreak. Their suicidal daylight raids, with bomb-loads far lighter than the monsters designed for British heavy bombers by Barnes Wallis, inspired this ditty (to the tune of *John Brown's Body*):

> *Forty Flying Fortresses at forty fousand feet*
> *Forty Flying Fortresses at forty fousand feet*
> *Forty Flying Fortresses at forty fousand feet*
> *But they've only got a teeny weeny bomb*

Their quasi-religious term of 'mission' for a bombing operation was generally felt to be in poor taste (it's general now!), and newsreel shots of priestly blessings of those about to take off to plaster Germany with high explosives would sometimes provoke cat-calls from station cinema audiences.

Canadians were generally known as 'Cocksuckers', not (so far as I am aware) that they were thought to indulge in the practice, but because it was a favourite expletive as in, 'That cocksuckin' groundcrew forgot to clean out the Elsan.'

With the Poles, language was the main barrier – a tongue-twisting agglomeration of consonants which inhibited socialising. Also, the widespread ignorance at the time about Poland and the Poles gave rise to all sorts of myths, including the 'well-known fact' that passionate Poles were apt to bite off nipples in their sexual frenzy, though no one I knew could ever produce evidence of a nipplectomy.

With Czechs it was corsets. Pamela Gillilan again in *Bridlington* from *All Steel Traveller*:

> *A bow. You dance?*
> *One or two circuits.*
> *Then – You sleep with me?*
> *We could feel corset bones beneath*
> *The tailored uniforms, smell scent . . .*

Ah! You can't beat a nice smelly Englishman, preferably vegetarian!

I did make one attempt to breach the Polish wire. At a showing of *Dangerous Moonlight* in the camp cinema I found myself sitting next to a Polish flight sergeant wearing the metal aircrew badge which made it unclear – at least to my eyes – whether the wearer was a pilot or some other branch of aircrew, and which Alan called 'costume jewellery'.

In the film Anton Walbrook took the star part of a Polish piano-playing fighter pilot, though the real star was Richard Adinsall's tuneful theme music, the *Warsaw Concerto*, playing everywhere at the time and assumed by Nellie (and still today by many) to be a fully-fledged classical work – until I loftily put her right.

As the lights went up and everyone became upright for the King we exchanged grins. 'Flying bad, music good!' I volunteered in the pidgin mode I still tend to employ for foreigners and toddlers. He made a wry face: 'Music OK. Flying pees poor!' I nodded vigorously. Cat-calls and cries of, 'Get real,' had as usual accompanied the flying sequences – aircraft which were clearly models performing impossible manoeuvres to the banshee scream of wind-through-struts-and-wire, although they were monoplanes (it still goes on!).

'In my room – Chopin – gramophone – Pader*ew*ski' – I faltered, desperate for a follow-up before the blackout embraced us. A puzzled look quickly gave way to enlightenment. '*Evsky*,' he barked. '*Evsky*... Pader*evsky*!' I laughed off my slight embarrassment. 'My Polish not good.' Jabbing a finger into his chest he grinned, 'My English pees poor!'

Before we parted I invited him over to hear the Chopin on my wind-up, but he didn't respond and I never came across him again. Perhaps it was as well as the crew carapace was a fragile one, and consorting with a strange pilot might have been seen by the three Wop/Ags as disloyalty ('Still fancying yourself as a fighter boy?'). All the same, I have always regretted the lost opportunity to learn something of the nation's suffering at the hands of both Germans and Russians – which might have made me more vociferous about the scurvy treatment they received from us after the war.

Fuselage Fun

As with most wartime experiences, what abides is the companionship, humour, and a sort of irresponsibility engendered by the service life which stand out in contrast to the hard realities that had to be faced by most of us returning to civvy street at the war's end.

Life was a curious mixture of discipline and lawlessness. At Christmas 1943 Ron raided a nearby farm and returned with a cockerel, while in the following early summer we four NCOs returned to camp from a country ramble with a whole pile of mushrooms which someone had gathered and left under a tree for later collection, and which Clarice the cookhouse WAAF — she of the assignation in the dinghy-drill hangar — served up garnished with bacon and chips.

Above all, it was the long hours spent together in the air and dependence of each crew member on the efforts and skills of the others which was a special factor in the long-range air war.

There were, of course, moments of tension, and on a long trip tempers were sometimes on the short side, though always curried with humour. I have a clear recollection of an incident in which Stanley took umbrage over an accusation that he was smoking in the rear turret, a practice rightly frowned on by the RAF in any part of an aircraft, though the author of *No Place to Land* and his fellow Poles seem to have been aerial chain-smokers, as were most Americans.

The tail section was the Wellington's *anus horribilis*. At night it was a howling purgatory with the elevator and rudder cables jerking nakedly along the fuselage sides, underlining the aircraft's flimsy pedigree back through the Wellesley to the fabric and wire contraptions of the Great War. Even the geodetic framework, which in the forward part of the aircraft on a moonlight night could suggest cathedral tracery, here assumed a menacing aspect, skeletal reminder of the burnt-out airship R101 which Barnes Wallis had also had a hand in designing.

The rear turret was its cul-de-sac, at night a most inhospitable place, always in memory occupied by Stanley, who at least on warmer nights would resist as often as possible the shift changes with the other two Wop/Ags, neither of whom was a keen arse-end Charlie. Ron, as I have said, was expert on the centimetric radar, and Rex had become wedded to the wireless (on which he was a wizard) — sometimes, as I was passing along the fuselage, plugging me in to snatches of Mozart or Beethoven salvaged from the screaming cacophony of the ether. Alan, on one of his prowls to the rear during my spell in the cockpit, would express mild concern that the scheduled shift changes seemed not to be taking place regularly, but *laissez-faire* set in as the tour proceeded.

It was on a long, moonless and uneventful anti-submarine patrol over Biscay that I came near to surprising Stanley smoking a fag – I think all except Alan smoked. As usual, the passage down the fuselage would have been slow, with pauses to pump fuel from auxiliary to main tanks and victual navigator and wireless and radar operators – the routine tasks of a second dicky – and perhaps use the Elsan, though only for number one as potty-trained crews like ours made it a point of honour never, except in *extremis*, to 'move me bowels' when airborne.

A Wellington interior showing the Elsan lavatory

It may have been on this occasion that I found Rex nodding off at the radar, something he was apt to do in mid-trip, lulled by the phosphorescent strobe as it swept the screen. Lifting his helmet I would have shouted something like, 'Wakey-wakey! You've missed a U-boat, a Seine netter and Jesus walking the waves,' the shock of which would risk his contravening the Elsan rule.

The turret's steel doors, as welcoming as Traitors' Gate, would normally have been jerked open at my knock in eager expectation of rations, but on this occasion there was significant delay. When Stan's droopily moustached visage, framed in its Viking helmet, did appear it wore a startled expression, guilt almost. A lung-titillating burst of fresh cigarette smoke hit me, with underneath the ashy tang of a just-extinguished *doofer* (do-for-tomorrow). The scowl he directed at me as he turned from peering into the darkness hardly softened as he took the proffered coffee – I wondered if he'd burned fingers in his haste to douse the fag, fearing perhaps that it was the skipper on the prowl.

As I regarded him, hands cupped round the steaming mug, he seemed in the orange reflection of the gun-sight to have taken on the likeness of a night watchman crouched over his brazier. After squeaks from his earphones he pushed the empty mug at me. 'Don't get your cock trapped – I'm rotating to track that float.' Bob must have launched a flame-float down the midships flare chute and testily ordered Stan to give him a drift. It was now his task to train the gun-sight on the bobbing float, read off the degrees of drift indicated on the turret rim calibration, and pass the information forward to enable Bob to calculate wind speed and direction as an aid to checking our position.

His torch illuminated the calibration and I read his lips as he reported five degrees of starboard drift. Then, with a suddenness which made me start, the intercom plug was ripped from its socket and his teeth gnashed white in fury. 'Bloody drivers! Wants to know if anyone's been smoking.' (It is a curious fact that smells in the Wimpy drifted for'ard, against the wind as it were, which is one reason why we held our fire on the Elsan.) 'You can tell him that one more bleat and I'll turn the turret reciprocal,' (this would have been impossible) 'and give him a burst up the arse.' With this, the doors clacked to, though not before his Parthian shot: 'Pilots? I've shit better!'

I decided to report negatively on the smoking question on my return to the cockpit should Alan ask. He didn't, which surprised me slightly as he had laid down the anti-smoking policy at OTU, being scathing about the lax discipline of American aviators, whom he accused of going into battle chomping cigars as well as swamping the airwaves with loose R/T (radio telephone) natter of the 'Rodger dodger over-and-out' variety.

Climbing over the main wing spar on my way back to the cockpit, the thought hit me: 'He didn't have his sandwiches!' I carried on, unable to face turning back. After all these years I remember the feeling of guilt. On a long trip one looked forward to coffee and a wad as eagerly as a bored housewife to her elevenses.

* * *

With approaching spring came brighter weather and, as if to celebrate, we stitched beneath our aircrew brevets the red, white and blue ribbon of the 1939-43 Star, awarded to those in the three services on active service during that period, and derisively christened 'Spam Medal'. (The qualifying period was later extended to VJ Day 1945.)

In further celebration, the squadron flew a series of 'daylights', on one of these being briefed to support Sunderlands which had been alerted to deal with a reported mid-Bay concentration of U-boats. As so often, we encountered nothing, failing even to make contact with the flying boats, which was a pity as they were an impressive sight, their streaked white bulk demoting the Wimpy from whale to dolphin, although it was pleasant squaring the visible ocean, clocking up easy hours towards the tour total.

Alan, alerted at briefing to patrol activity by the JU88 outfit near Lorient, hugged the cloud base ready for hide-and-seek should the worst happen.

I thought at one point that it had. Passing aft for some reason I lingered at the astrodome, dreamily scanning the grey-green fusion of sea and sky, when I spotted a black dot against the silver fringe of cloud to starboard. Christ! An aircraft, approaching on a beam attack course! Dry mouth, thumping heart, click on: 'Second pilot from astro dome. Aircraft ninety degrees, closing . . .'

What devil drove me to say this, and having said it kept me from uttering an instant retraction? For I had realised in the act of clicking on that we were under attack from nothing more dangerous than a spot of oil which had blown back from the starboard engine onto the perspex dome. A sadistic urge to test Alan's nerve? A sudden impulse to make something – anything – happen to relieve the tedium?

Something certainly happened. The aircraft lunged into a diving starboard turn so steep and sudden that I lost my footing. Falling, I saw Bob's charts, instruments and beaker of coffee in mid-air as dust rained down from the deck (which now aspired to be the ceiling). Alan was executing the classic corkscrew manoeuvre for avoiding enemy aircraft fire.

Bob crawled towards me as I lay spreadeagled, his face a map of anger. 'What the hell's he doing, screwing around the sky like this? My plot's all f***ed up – he can find his own goddam way back!'

The aircraft was now in a climbing turn to port and, struggling to my feet, I saw that we were just entering the cloud base. Plugging in, I reported no aircraft in sight before collapsing in a helpless bout of laughter. Rex and Ron stared at me from their positions at the beam scare guns they had manned, God knew how, as part of the enemy aircraft drill, while Bob stuck his face into mine, demanding to know what was going on.

Between gasps I told him, whereupon the mask cracked and he doubled up, cackling uncontrollably, using my Mae West as a punch-bag before staggering back to his position where he collapsed into the shambles.

Of course, I owned up, and such was Alan's relief that he laughed it off, probably aware that corkscrewing rather than instantly climbing into cloud cover might have given an oil spot with canon-bearing wings the chance to make mischief. The rest of the crew never let me forget it.

Western Approaches

The entries for November 1943 recall that for three weeks we were based at St Eval in Cornwall while the runways at Chivenor were being repaired. This was a long-range Liberator and Fleet Air Arm station, and is remembered with gratitude for the generous tots of rum dispensed on our return from exhausting trips over Biscay and the Atlantic. Ron, Rex, Stan and I occupied billets in the small village of St Columb, and it was there at a village dance that Rex met the Land Army girl who soon became his wife, Bob and I attending the wedding in Somerset.

January/February 1944 saw us diverted for three weeks to Limavady in Northern Ireland, a Coastal Command airfield just south of Lough Foyle, the almost enclosed body of water through which, I seemed to recall, King Billy's ships had sailed to the relief of Londonderry in God-knows-when. From there we were to patrol the North-West Approaches where, it was presumed, there was more submarine activity than in the Bay, though I recall only one successful attack by a 612 crew during our stay. What I do remember is the unbelievable greenness of the landscape. It was the iridescence of those glossy pre-war birthday cards in which the emerald green smudged over the outlines of grass and leaves surrounding the lipstick-red roses.

At about this time I learned of Dick's demise over Duisberg, and remember crooning to myself '*And only man is vile*' as I looked down on the Giant's Causeway, castle ruins, squat white cottages and neat villages strung along the north coast as far as Londonderry and Ballykelly.

The dominating feature of our immediate landscape was the 'Goddam mountain' which Bob had pointed out on the map when news of the posting had come through. This was Binevenagh, at whose foot the airfield spread itself. Benevolent when its back was bathed in sunshine, it became a crouching beast on a dirty night or in daytime fog, ready to reach out and clutch a straying aircraft in the manner of King Kong atop the Empire State Building. Alan worried away at the topography, learning by heart the correct approaches to the runways from seaward in all conditions of wind and weather. It was the contained worry of a man reprieved from hanging, making the best of a life sentence with some expectation of remission if Hitler's luck continued to run out.

On one particularly dirty night after a bumpy final approach and ropey landing in a heavy cross-wind, Stanley, drawing heavily on his 'first fag since take-off' muttered memorably that he thought we were going to 'scrape the goat shit off the mountain!' My somewhat cavalier dismissal of the hazard was cured when later in the year I returned to Limavady as a skipper. Blind flying in mountainous areas was my worst nightmare – the Duke of Kent's demise in a Sunderland which hit a Scottish mountain made a big impression on me too!

My personal strikes were against golf balls on a course overlooking the Irish Sea – which showed such promise that I decided never to play again, a resolution I've kept and never regretted. On one occasion bad weather diverted us to an airstrip on the Hebridean island of Tiree where, according to the corporal who guided us to dispersal, the only sexual opportunities were provided by the sheep, for which encounters one wore wellingtons into which the back legs could be tucked.

Although the airborne action was minimal there was a fascinating development on the ground. This was to do with the Tannoy system which, as on all RAF airfields, blared forth stomach-tightening messages of the *'Corporal Podwell to report to the guard-room immediately'* variety – the Big Brother later immortalised in Orwell's *1984*.

What distinguished the Limavady Tannoy from others was that the duty controller on the speaking end would use Rossini's *The Thieving Magpie* overture as a morning wakey-wakey call. An urge to meet this *rara avis* was frustrated by the dispersal of the constituent elements of the station – which had been taken to absurd lengths. The sergeants mess was half a mile from the ops block, while the various living quarters were flung carelessly about Binevenagh's feet. The sick bay we never did find, so forged the signatures on our FFI (Free From Infection) chits. And all this though it was rumoured that the only bombs which had fallen within miles of the airfield had been excreted by a panic-stricken Whitley lost in a fog early in the war.

The mystery of the music-loving Tannoy man was solved many years later by an obituary in the *Independent*. The voice had belonged to one Stafford Cottman who had died in Bath on 19 September 1999, having lived with his wife for some years within a mile or so of the village in which I'd been anchored for a decade. He'd been the youngest of Orwell's comrades in the Spanish Civil War and is one of the small group pictured in my Folio edition of Orwell's *Homage to Catalonia* – dwarfed as they were by the great man's gangling frame.

As well as unmasking him as the musical Tannoyist, the obituary revealed that, after becoming a conscientious objector in token protest at the pre-war government's failure to support the Republican cause, he had joined the RAF as an air gunner, surviving a tour of operations in Bomber Command only because a burst eardrum prevented his flying on the last trip, from which his comrades never returned – the spare bod syndrome again.

I telephoned his widow, who told me that their daughter, a consultant psychiatrist, had just moved to my village, and shortly afterwards I met them both. They were able to fill me in on other aspects of 'Staff's' life, including photographs showing him as a much smarter looking airman than I ever was. It saddens me to think of the lost opportunity of meeting one who, as well as embodying many of the qualities and political views I admire, could endlessly have fed my obsession with Orwell and the war in Spain which had so coloured my adolescence. While I and countless others had fantasised about joining the volunteers, 'Staff' had actually done it.

E-Boats

Passing down the Irish Sea in early March 1944 on the squadron's mass return to Chivenor, we overhauled a Short Stirling – huge and blackly menacing in a way which the designers of the Lancaster and Halifax had managed to avoid. I was driving, and in my cheerful way waved as we passed to starboard. The only response was a shallow turn to port, the aeronautical equivalent of a snub, which released an unreasoning gush of hatred for the snubber. All my doubts about the moral and strategic justification for Harris's area bombing campaign with its mounting toll of aircrew – now including Dick – were concentrated on this flying coffin, slipping away bearing my curse.

The contrast, as I caught up with the Wimpy piloted by John Perry, a popular but outspoken NCO skipper, restored the good feeling I'd had about the return to Chivenor, his exaggerated wing-waggle as eloquent a greeting as a backslap. John had achieved notoriety shortly before the secondment to Ireland on being shot up by a German E-boat when on a non-operational daytime flight over the Scilly Isles. I have never forgotten his indignation when describing the incident: 'The cheeky sod! Shot through the wing-root – in my own back yard!' Doubtless, in response to his 'Mayday', Beaufighters from a nearby base would have been scrambled to deal with the intruder, though we heard nothing more of the incident.

Having shot their bolt with both pocket and full-sized battleships, the Kriegsmarine were now deploying these small but well-armed and very fast boats in hit-and-run raids against our coastal shipping and harbours in what everyone assumed to be the run-up to the opening of a Second Front, for which Uncle Joe, as Roosevelt had dubbed the murderous betrayer of Dick's socialist principles, had long been pressing.

I don't recall any further E-boat sightings by 612 aircraft, but a couple of months after our return they played a leading part in a second-front training exercise which went badly wrong – again in our back yard. Because of strict secrecy surrounding the run-up to D-Day we knew nothing about it then or for years afterwards. The incident merged with the high drama of D-Day itself (which occurred a week later), and the full story took many years to emerge.

The *locus in quo* – a term which seems appropriate for what amounted to a criminally botched exercise – was Lyme Bay, some twelve miles south-south-east of Chivenor, selected because the beach known as Slapton Sands was topographically similar to Utah Beach in Normandy (where the Americans were due to land on D-Day). About three thousand residents in the area surrounding the beach, some of whom had never before left their village, had been evacuated on safety grounds and to preserve secrecy.

For some time before our stint in Northern Ireland we'd been aware of growing American military activity in our part of Devon, but from early in 1944 Lyme Bay and Slapton Sands seemed generally to be off-limits for over-flying aircraft, though I recollect that it was on an earlier training exercise somewhere in the area that I'd witnessed a scene which has remained with me: an armada of toy landing craft approaching the wide sweep of golden sands, each at the apex of a V, water beetles on a breeze-swept pond.

The scene during the small hours of 28 April was as far removed from that as hell from heaven. In an operation code-named *Exercise Tiger* a string of eight Landing Ship Tanks (LSTs) carrying vehicles and American combat engineers *en route* to practise a beach landing, inadequately protected by the Royal Navy, was attacked by a force of nine E-boats. In the ensuing mayhem over six hundred soldiers and sailors were lost, and when the surviving LSTs made it to Slapton a further three hundred-odd men died from so-called 'friendly fire'. To harden them by exposure to real battle conditions it had been arranged that a British battleship would shell the landing area as the LSTs approached, the occupants not to advance beyond a white tape on the beach until the shelling had ceased. In the confusion this was disregarded and the mayhem occurred.

The botched tactics, poor communications and general muddle make sad reading. Perhaps lessons were learned as the casualties during the landing on Utah Beach were far fewer than those in what came to be known as 'The Battle of Lyme Bay'.

Why the three Chivenor squadrons – or others on surrounding airfields – were not mobilised to provide air cover for the exercise, I can't think, though maybe it was the old story of inter-service rivalry. 'This is a Royal Navy show – we'll protect the Yanks ourselves, thank you, and don't want the RAF putting their oar in!'

D-Days

Day One: 23 May 1944

Although the date for the invasion of France was a closely-guarded and well-kept secret there were many signs as spring merged into early summer that it was imminent, and this, with the continuing successes on the Russian Front, gave one the absurd notion that the war's end might not be long delayed, which in turn raised the probability of an early return to civvy street.

The girl Ronald and I had encountered on one of our pre-war sweeps of the toffier districts of Leicester now wore the engagement ring which Nellie and my sisters had nudged me into buying, and with Rex's marriage and the impression Betty had made on the crew when she came down for a weekend ('For God's sake, Bill, what are you waiting for? If you don't, someone else will!'), the pressure to name the day became almost irresistible. She was serving in the operations room of the National Fire Service in Leicester, and when my next leave coincided with her tour of duty I realised that she had many admiring male colleagues, so I stopped havering and we fixed the twenty-third of May for our marriage (to coincide with my next fourteen-day aircrew leave).

Betty's father had died some years previously and her two soldier brothers were serving abroad, one in Burma, the other in North Africa, so Phil's father Dick readily agreed to perform that odd ritual of giving the bride away. Stan was my best man, and Nellie conjured up a respectable reception at *Greyfell* following the wedding at Braunstone church, my future mother-in-law raising no objection at being relieved of the customary obligation of the bride's parents to, as Hamlet put it, *furnish forth the marriage tables.*

The honeymoon was soon settled. Wop/Ag Ron had been given permission to 'live out' from our Chivenor base, and his wife and small daughter had exchanged bomb-scarred London for a furnished chalet at nearby Croyde, part of a holiday camp run before the war by NALGO (National Association of Local Government Officers), the trade union to which I belonged. I too obtained living-out consent, and after the wedding Betty and I took up residence in an adjacent chalet.

Wedding line-up, including Mildred, Stan, the author, Betty, & Phil's father

It was a magical time. After my leave ended and flying recommenced, Ron and I would usually cycle the few miles to Croyde and stretch out in the early summer sunshine after supplementing the ops breakfast with whatever the girls had rustled up. Then, depending on the weather, Betty and I would amble off for a walk along the cliffs at Croyde Bay or to the beach for a swim.

I found it remarkable to be living in a chalet which might have been occupied pre-war by the County Clerk, Lucas E Rumsey, or Dick (both having been enthusiastic holidaymakers at Croyde Bay). I remember Dick expressing his astonishment at Lucas E's participation in such larks as *Underneath the Spreading Chestnut Tree*, a happy-clappy routine which had been much enjoyed in Scout camps by the

King when Duke of York. I myself found it difficult to imagine Dick letting down his stiffly sprouting grey hair among frolicking junior clerks, even though he had mellowed to the extent that when he died of a heart attack in the sixties it was in front of the television chuckling at 'Mr Pastry', an amiable comedian popular in those innocent days. (Having now turned ninety I try to avoid watching anything which might embarrass those left behind should I similarly expire – which severely limits my time before the small screen.)

Mona, a darkly handsome woman with two young daughters, lived in a house near the chalets and we became great friends. She was an exceptional cook, though it was not advisable to inspect too closely the contents of the pans and pots in her kitchen. Husband Norton was a navigator on Mosquitos who later earned a DFC. One night, Mona knocked on our window in the small hours to say that he'd arrived home on a short leave and would we join them for a drink and to hear a Brahms recording he'd acquired? As the next day was a 'stand down' the marital bed was readily vacated. This friendship lasted for many years, and it was with them that we first heard Britten's *War Requiem*.

Day Two: 6 June 1944

The Air Commodore from 19 Group who addressed us, slim and immaculate, though not over-tall, bore some resemblance to Air Chief Marshal Tedder of the second Tactical Air Force (in one of whose Typhoons I should by rights have been flying over Normandy). His tailored, chest-hugging blouse negated its description as 'battledress', though the row of fruit salad below the wings (including the DFC) attested to his participation in some sort of battle. The contrast with the dusty blue sloppiness of the aircrew lapping round him to hear the Sermon on the Mount was startling.

'I want every man of you,' he was barking into the fresh south-westerly, 'to keen yourselves up all round. Take risks, go over to the attack whenever the enemy exposes himself . . .' (my glance intercepted Bob's and where they met appeared a hologram – word not yet in common use or even, perhaps, invented – of a deckful of U-boaters dropping their trousers in defiance as the Leigh Light beam caught them on deck taking the night air) '. . . and also bang on time. Patrols will be flown with clockwork precision. They've been worked out to cover every inch of the Bay and Channel by day and night . . . twenty-four hours. A five-minute error might mean a U-boat slipping through the net, so any slackness will not, repeat not, be tolerated.'

Ah! The threat! After the 'you chaps, good shows, waccos and bang-ons' came always the threat!

There was more, concluding with: 'Well, that's it. Go to it and keep at it until Winston's got Hitler's remaining ball as a watch-fob' (Laughter). He leaped nimbly into the sea of blue which became a stream flowing away from the hangars. As if on cue, a Wimpy swept low on its final approach, the black invasion stripes transmogrifying it from ageing sea cow to frisky zebra, and finally, as it pounced on the runway, to bird of prey.

We then received a general briefing on the D-Day operation and details of the frequency and patterns of our patrols, with such intelligence as there was on expected U-boat activity. It looked as if our particular patrolling would be well south of the cross-Channel invasion route, but the fact that we would be within spitting distance of the action was mildly exciting.

The excitement was heightened when we were each issued with a revolver, holster and gun-belt, seemingly of Great War vintage, which transformed the impressionable into swaggering cowboys – a reminder that the school playground was still fresh in the memory of many. I don't recall anyone explaining how we were to deploy these side-arms over the Bay, the inference being that if things didn't go well with the landings we might be flung into the land battle!

The highly charged atmosphere survived even the air test, briefing and other pre-operational rituals which preceded our evening departure on the first of the three 'post D-Day' patrols in which I took part. When we were shot into the evening sky on the first trip by the controller's Very pistol with Group Captain Chilton, the kindly station commander, and other top brass lining the control tower platform, the outside chance that we might see action hardened into virtual certainty.

Of course, we didn't. Not surprisingly – long after the war's end I learned that not a single U-boat penetrated the English Channel during the D-Day operation. The last three entries in the log book covering my time at Chivenor were as blandly undramatic as the rest:

```
June 9    A/S patrol English Channel  5.30 hrs Day 4.30 Night
 "   14       "        "       "      4.30     "   5.30   "
 "   27       "        "       "      5.35     "   5.00   "
```

Finis! No mention of having witnessed any part of an updated Prologue to Act Three of Henry V:

> *. . . oh do but think*
> *You stand upon the ravage and behold*
> *A city on th'inconstant billows dancing;*
> *For so appears this fleet majestical . . .*

I have searched the furthest recesses of memory in an effort to recall anything which during these last patrols hinted even vaguely at the scenes of great pith and moment which were being enacted so near to us, but the turbulent waters of the Bay stretched grey to the horizon, darkening with the fading of the light as the hours wore away.

I don't recall any great sense of disappointment, perhaps because it was at this time that Alan broke the news of my posting to a captain's course at No 6 (Coastal) OTU near Silloth on the Solway Firth in Cumberland, giving me much to think about. For an undemonstrative type he seemed surprisingly affected, though any break-up of a seasoned crew was looked upon with a mixture of the sweet sorrow of parting and fear that the change might bring bad luck.

The brief *fête champêtre* at Croyde had come to an end, and Betty was now back in Leicester living with her mother. The nine months based at Chivenor with the short period of living-out had acquired an almost domestic quality which was unlikely to be matched on any future station, and when I look back over the almost seventy years since the three Wop/Ags cycled with me to the railway station on their creaking service bikes, Rex insisting on balancing my kitbag precariously on his handlebars, it is the quality of their companionship that I remember – in the air, in the winter comfort of our billet with its central stove, in the mess ante-room playing noisy matches on the rackety football game, in our explorations of the summer pastures surrounding the airfield, and on our bikes in line astern after a session in the Flying Fox, hurtling downhill emptying imaginary Brownings into a fleeing JU88 . . .

Alan and Bob arrived as the train drew in but left before its delayed departure. Stan, Rex and Ron stood waving until a curve in the line disappeared them.

Though I didn't know it I'd also seen the last of the *Bay of Whiskey* – our future hunting ground would be the Irish Sea, North Atlantic and Western approaches. There were few regrets. It was all very well braving wind, weather and weariness while there was still the ghost of a chance of finding a target, but with the Allies now within reach of the U-boat bases on the French coast the Battle of the Bay was as good as over.

Hudson Bay

The Solway Firth, on the left side of the Kingdom, had been renamed Hudson Bay earlier in the war for the number of Lockheed Hudson aircraft which had found a watery grave beneath its surface, when that American military conversion of a passenger airliner had been one of Coastal's early workhorses.

The Yanks were crafty in anticipating the post-war requirement for passenger and transport aircraft. The DC3 Dakota, which had become the stalwart of Transport Command, and which I was to fly after VE Day, switched effortlessly to a civilian role on the outbreak of peace, making mega-bucks for Lockheed and pioneering new international routes, whereas Britain struggled along with make-do civil versions of the Lancaster and Halifax until the new breed of civil aircraft flew off the drawing boards. As ever, Uncle Sam was quick off the mark.

Before choosing a crew I had to demonstrate that I was competent to fly the Wimpy as first pilot, which I managed to do after three hours with an instructor. A pleasant course member, also a flight sergeant, shared the same shepherd, and after solo-ing we practised circuits and bumps in the same aircraft, afterwards continuing to carry out more advanced training together by day and night for almost a month, until the time came to crew-up.

Towards the end of our mutual training his commission came through, and I remember teasing him about the rigidity of his new service cap, suggesting he kick it around to make it more lived-in – as did I when, at the German war's end, I too achieved officer status (somewhat against my egalitarian principles).

The crewing-up procedure hadn't changed. Choosing rather than being chosen called for a more positive approach, but I was surprised how easily the Tory-leader magic worked, and the crew which coalesced around me remained unchanged until VE Day and the squadron's break-up: Harry, an assertive Geordie, was my second pilot; Joe, a peacetime NCO who had remustered to aircrew, the navigator; and Paddy, Hedley and Louis Wop/Ags (respectively Irish leprechaun, London cockney and handsome Mauritian).

Within days of achieving his commission, my new friend died with his crew when an engine failed on a night take-off – always a critical time. I can still see the tall tail-fin of the burnt out aircraft standing erect beyond the runway's end in the morning, a memorial to the six young men setting out hopefully on their journey together. Another crew, skippered by an officer who seemed rather old for operational flying (thirty was getting on for 'past it') disappeared one night over the Firth – these, I think, were the only casualties.

The course was unusually long (six weeks compared with the three at Haverfordwest), necessary because of the developments in the anti-submarine war which called for new tactics and familiarity with the latest products of the back-room boys. The main advance on the German side had seen the replacement of many of the old-type U-boats by a new marque fitted with the Schnorkel – a pipe which allowed them to 'breathe' while submerged – and other refinements.

If, in an ultra-calm sea, a Schnorkeller were detected but disappeared beneath the surface, it might be possible to depth-charge it by tracing its course and depth with a pattern of sonar buoys, a complicated procedure in which Mr Carter's mathematics would be useful.

Judging by those round the Firth, calm seas might be a rarity, but our hope was that the strained resources of the Third Reich in its death throes might have delayed the full implementation of the replacement programme. It was therefore with some prospect of action that 'Self and Crew' settled down to serious flying and earnest study of the new techniques, and by the end of the course we had achieved the goal of operating as a single entity with confidence in each other's ability.

The concentrated activity left little time for exploring the surrounds of the airfield and I don't remember putting a foot in Silloth itself, which is a pity as I later learned that Kathleen Ferrier (the contralto) had lived there, she whose recordings of *Blow the Wind Southerly* and *Lied von der Erde* always bring a tear.

The one or two expeditions to nearby Carlisle didn't impress, perhaps because we were made aware that the absenteeism of the city's factory workers during the Great War had led the government to introduce the restriction of pub opening hours as a temporary measure – which of course became permanent and general. Oh, city of the damned!

After end-of-course leave we were to report in October to 172 Leigh Light Wellington Squadron at Limavady, familiar to me through our brief detachment there from Chivenor. I recalled with a slight chill the difficulty Alan had experienced on night landings in bad weather under the beetling brow of Binevenagh, and recalled Stan's *goat-shit* remark as he took his first drag at a fag after a tricky landing.

'Oh, his offence is rank!'

At about this time my promotion to Warrant Officer appeared on Daily Routine Orders – a rank often regarded as the best in the RAF since you were top dog among the NCOs without having surrendered the last vestiges of proletarianism, and (more importantly) with none of the mess bills that went with a commission. The rank badges which replaced the Flight Sergeant's chevrons and crown were indeed known as 'dogs' – though not 'top' as they were worn lower down the arm (as if distancing themselves from the 'shitehawks' which had roosted on each tunic shoulder in my previous ranks).

The quotation from *Hamlet* in the heading appeared below a caricatured Air Marshal in an edition of the wartime magazine, *Tee Emm* – short for Technical Magazine – published by the Air Ministry as a fairly light-hearted way of keeping its airmen and women in touch with such technical information as was not secret, at the same time as commending good practices in the air and on the ground.

The editors presumably took for granted that many of its readers would make the connection with Hamlet's comment on his stepfather – unless of course they were simply indulging themselves. It still surprises me that this and other assumptions should have been made in a technical publication aimed at members of a service, most of whom would have received only a basic secondary education.

A welcome addition to the dog-eared flying magazines in the mess ante-room, *Tee Emm's* technical articles were relieved by humour, the cartoon character P/O Prune's appalling airmanship highlighting the growing number of wartime flying accidents. Hanging by his straps when looping the loop (having neglected properly to fasten the safety harness) was a typical Prunism, while a remembered cartoon had an irate landowner, narrowly missed by the trailing wireless aerial which Prune had forgotten to reel in before landing, exclaiming, '*Gad, sir, I'm being shot at!*'

It was the Air Marshal cartoon which first made me question the nomenclature of commissioned ranks in the RAF. Whereas an NCO's rank gave no clue to his function (a flight sergeant, for instance, might be a pilot or the 'chiefy' in charge of servicing his aircraft), I began to find it absurd to call a newly-commissioned airman *Pilot Officer* regardless of whether he was qualified to fly an aircraft or a desk, and to carry this on through Flying Officer, Flight Lieutenant, Squadron Leader, Wing Commander and Group Captain. From Air

Commodore to Marshall of the Royal Air Force the flying connotation was perhaps less misleading, though jokers were known to suggest that the former might be best qualified to pilot a commode.

Of course, the difficulties faced in 1918 by Trenchard and the politicians in coming up with suitable rank designations were formidable. They had to make it plain that the new force would be independent of the army and navy, from whose air arms it was being snatched, while avoiding a multiplicity of titles indicating specific skills, whether ground- or air-based. The Americans, in giving their ground-based air arm virtual independence during the second world war, chose to retain army ranks, so avoiding the pejorative terms 'wingless wonder' or 'penguin', often employed by RAF aircrew to distinguish themselves from non-flying officers.

There was to me a sense of apartheid in relations between flying and non-flying airmen, though I believe it was less apparent during peacetime – when Trenchard's rigid standards for the training of groundcrew gave apprentices a pride in their skills to set against the more leisurely accomplishments of the aviators. But as the pre-war trickle of aircrew became a flood I sensed that the status of non-aviators in both officers and sergeants messes diminished as standards declined and peacetime privileges disappeared.

I'd had a taste of how it had been on my short *beam approach* course on a small airfield in Cheshire, where the trainees were outnumbered by permanent staff. Corporal waiters served food at formal meals in the sergeants mess, where best blue was *de rigueur*, a world away from the self-service mealtime scrambles at Chivenor. I had the feeling that if any course member had been heard to refer to a non-flying man in a pejorative way he would have been barred from the mess, or even put on a charge!

Back to Binevenagh

My new outfit, 172 Squadron, had been one of the most successful of the Biscay sub-hunters in the glory days following the introduction of the Leigh Light, but Northern Ireland was hardly the soft underbelly of the Axis and I couldn't imagine that many potential targets for our finely-honed skills would be lurking beneath the waves which washed its shores. Patrolling the Western Approaches, Irish Sea and the Atlantic coast of Eire may still have been necessary – throughout the war it was suspected that elements in the neutral Republic were giving comfort to the enemy and it was only recently that my own suspicions were laid to rest. In an authoritative study, *In Time of War (Ireland, Ulster and the Price of neutrality 1939-45* by Robert Fisk, the *Independent* newspaper's foreign correspondent makes it abundantly clear that during the conflict the wartime administrations of de Valera, the Irish Taoiseach, tied themselves in knots to avoid suspicion of partiality towards *any* of the combatants – especially in the UK.

172 Squadron badge

But there must have been a more active role for us. There nearly was. On arrival, we were met with the *pukka gen* that the squadron was to be transferred immediately to a base on the Lincolnshire coast, with the agreeable task of attacking surface vessels off the Dutch coast. Visions of turning the stolid Wimpy into a *faux*-Beaufighter with a clutch of bombs or rockets substituted for depth charges – which indeed bore some resemblance to drumfuls of paint – re-awakened some of the *joie d'aviation* which the RAF had been steadily eroding since Harvard Heaven.

The next surprise was the arrival of 612 Squadron, as we assumed, to take over our patrolling routines. Whilst it was good to see Alan, Bob and the three Wop/Ags, I felt a pang of resentment on being introduced to the new second dicky, an F/O, who appeared to have been accepted as an adequate substitute for me. When he made to lift me off the ground to assess my suitability as a fly-half (whatever that was) resentment turned to sadness that my ex-comrades should have to tolerate such a bore. I couldn't, for instance, imagine him taking the mickey out of Rex nodding off at the radar, or joining in the pre-op dance routine.

The gen on the posting to the East Coast turned out to be duff – or perhaps there had been a last-minute change of plan. It was now 612 who were to go, news which may not have been received with transports of delight by some of the old stagers – including Alan – who had probably been stoically facing the prospect of a quiet end to their war.

I later learned that the squadron enjoyed little success as by that stage of the war there was little enemy shipping, but even so I couldn't bring myself to thank God for stepping in, however well-intentioned, to preserve me for the perils of peace by robbing me of the chance to end my war within the main theatre. I didn't join those lining the runway to see my old squadron's departure.

Our first flight together on 172 – a training flight – was on 23 November 1944. Our last operational flight, on 28 May 1945, was a nine-hour trip in the North Atlantic escorting a convoy which included the SS Mauretania, by which time we had completed just over 200 operational hours with not so much as a grunt from a Schnorkell. We had begun to wonder whether the Grand Admiral had anticipated the end by ordering all his boats home.

The mixture was much as it had always been – battling through atrocious weather, nursing war-weary engines, returning to base early if things got too bad, and coping with the additional hazard of skirting the mountain on night landings. Patrols in the Irish Sea were especially hazardous as on a stormy night a naval sloop presented a radar image easily mistaken for a submarine. In the Bay there had been no such problem, the nocturnal waters being innocent of Allied vessels so that anything on the surface was fair game.

Author and crew, 172 Squadron

Some years ago, on reading an account by Sir Ludovic Kennedy of wartime experiences in the Irish Sea, I wrote to ask him if his was the vessel we illuminated one night as, if so, I would like to thank him for not firing first and asking questions afterwards. His friendly reply was in the negative.

I see that on a daylight patrol in April we had a bit of fun attacking a floating mine with depth charges and machine-gun fire to prevent its becoming a hazard to our shipping. Disappointingly, although it disappeared beneath the waves there was no spectacular explosion – such as had illuminated my school firework display.

A pleasant diversion from the long patrols came with a train trip by self and crew to the Clyde for an RAF/RN liaison exercise, chiefly involving visits to a sub-hunting corvette and a Western Approaches operational centre. These were well-lubricated with Navy rum, and before returning we managed a short visit to Glasgow where, strolling along Sauchiehall Street, we came upon an amusement arcade. Inside, among the pinball and other cash-extracting machines was a sculpture in marble of a recumbent Christ bearing the legend: *Consumatum es. By Jacob Epstein.* I have often wondered how it came to be there – evacuated during the Blitz, I suppose, along with the children.

On 23 May my log book entry reads:

```
A/U Patrol: Blue Line North: 7.30 hours Day; 2 hours Night
```

These patrols marked the effective end of the war and followed the Grand Admiral's ordering German U-boat commanders to surrender at a given time. It was decreed that they should surface along two lines – *Blue Line North* in the Western Approaches and *Blue Line South* on the Biscay side.

Considering their virtual invisibility it was surprising how many popped up at the appointed time. The main impression on viewing the slim shapes from above was of how insignificant they looked, more suited to a municipal boating lake than to the limitless ocean – like Grandpa Tom's substitute for my lost-at-sea liner! They were escorted, in the case of BL North, to a Londonderry dockyard, where their crestfallen crews – perhaps secretly relieved – were interned. There the vessels remain, greyly despondent, in the buffalo skin-covered photograph album.

There was nothing in the way of Mafeking-euphoria as the news spread that VE Day would be on 8 June. Reactions were very much as those we had read about the Great Warriors on November 11 1918 – a dazed awareness that now it was all over the future would be in our own hands, not those of the unseen movers we had been able to blame for the last few years' adversities (yet had relied on for bed, board, transportation and regular paid holidays!).

Surrendered U-boats, Northern Ireland 1945

For my part there was the prospect of fatherhood as our first child was expected in July, and the question of where we would live was already exercising our minds. Although Betty was at present comfortably installed in her mother's house, her two brothers were likely to be among the first to be demobilised. Under her guidance I acquired quantities of ration-free Irish linen and other household goods unobtainable on the mainland.

And what would I do for a living? Would it be a case of 'What'cha gonna do with them down on the farm now that they've seen Pareee?' Would I forget the flying life and settle down tethered to a desk like the Harrogate squadron leader, 'Pegasus knackered'? *Gen* seeping through about the possibility of university or teacher-training college grants for returning servicemen brought realisation of the limiting effect of marriage and parenthood.

The Benevolent Mountain

Our last flight together on 31 May is entered as '`T.T.B 45 minutes: Day`'. What in God's name could that have been? And what a way to end 442.20 hours of operational flying: *Not with a bang but a Wimpy!*

I was surprised at how quickly the 'crew bond' loosened when flying stopped. Freed from the constant round of training, flight tests, briefings and ops, a collective sigh of relief seemed to ascend from the airfield to meet the mountain mists. The Wop/Ags spent much time at the butts, their targets now notional Japanese Zeros, while Harry and Joe became addicted to films at a Londonderry flea-pit, and Paddy made off home to Belfast whenever he could.

I took to the mountain, whose network of paths looked as if they might lead by easy stages to the summit from where, Godlike, I could survey land and seascape and pronounce the earth good – something to enjoy rather than a map or chart marked with course and track leading from A to B – at least until, after the customary rest, the Pacific beckoned.

It was a surprise on one of these walks to be confronted, on rounding a sharp bend, by a tall WAAF – one of the Ops Room girls, of whom the more glamorous were still lusted over at briefings. Although striking in appearance, she was not one of these. The heavy-lidded eyes in her pale face could have been looking down from the staircase of a crumbling mansion of the Anglo-Irish Ascendancy (which I later gathered was pretty much her background). We descended together and parted well short of her quarters in some remote grove, after arranging to meet again.

I think it appropriate to record here that there was no carnality in our brief association. The one moment – a long one – of physical proximity came after our last, extended walk, when suddenly in the darkness outside her quarters I found her head on my shoulder, a silent token of regret at our parting. My arms encircled her, feeling the tautness of her body, and I have never forgotten her.

It was now June, the long days were full of sunshine, and a happily conjunctive weekend off-duty allowed us to plan a longer than usual exploration of the mountain. At the summit, as we sat admiring the view over the Loch, a Fleet Air Arm *Stringbag* – Fairey Swordfish – clattered by level with us, the crew of three waving from the bi-plane's open cockpits as if returning thirty years late from a reconnaissance flight over the Somme.

Returning by a different route we looked for a shady spot where we could sit and eat the emergency flying rations I'd brought with me – chocolate, boiled sweets, Horlicks tablets – and the fresh fruit she'd hoarded. The path broadened, levelled out, and rounding a bend we came upon a squat, whitewashed cottage, its back against the rock face. The stable-type door was ajar and on the step sat a barefoot toddler in rough rompers. Startled, it disappeared inside. There was a burst of crying and then a woman (thirtyish, sturdy, with bird-bright eyes) emerged carrying the child. 'Hello, now.'

Advancing cautiously, I produced a bar of blended chocolate (milk was a war casualty) and offered it to the little boy, whose dimpled hand advanced towards it like a charmer's snake, took it and recoiled, his blue eyes all the while fixed on mine.

'You don't mind, do you?'

'I do not! It's little enough he sees of that these days.' She scraped at the dark, straight hair, and smoothed the Hessian apron.

'Look, I've got some sweets here and a bit more chocolate. Will you take them? We get more than we can do with.'

She nodded, and I saw in her eyes awareness of the wicked waste which went on below. 'Will you come in then?'

A quick glance at Margaret surprised a hesitant frown. Hell, I thought, she's visiting the peasantry. Nettled, I accepted the invitation. Inside, the room was dark, cool, and pungent with turf smoke. I laid my offering on the scrubbed table as mugs of strong tea were placed before us with a plate of homemade biscuits.

We didn't stay long. Margaret seemed uncomfortable in what I supposed she would have called a *cabin*. 'Snobbish bugger,' I thought, and made a point of promising to return with more spoils from below.

I'd done her an injustice. On the way down she explained that in her patch of rural Ireland it wasn't done to call casually other than on relatives or close friends. She'd felt embarrassed for the woman – in her working clothes and with an unwashed child.

Nevertheless, she not only joined me on my next jaunt but also brought her own sweet and cigarette rations and a woolly toy. This time, as we entered the dark room our nostrils encountered the tang of turf-smoked bacon. Mrs Claffey's sharp eyes detected my hungry glance at the frizzling contents of the big pan suspended over the fire. 'Wull you stop for a bite, muster, and the young lady?' I hesitated, glancing at Margaret. Misinterpreting my look, Mrs Claffey added: 'It's only rough food, now – nothing as fancy as you'll be getting down there.'

Down there! In this land of home-cured bacon, eggs galore and soda bread, the unpalatable RAF stodge that T E Lawrence had excoriated in *The Mint* still oozed out of greasy kitchens. I was now rarely eating in the mess, existing between operational meals on chocolate, fruit and strong Bruno tobacco.

The bacon and eggs from the pan measured up to the smell, and the bread was still warm from the oven. Margaret ate delicately but with relish after unostentatiously spreading a handkerchief over her best blue skirt. Mrs Claffey watched with satisfaction, asking questions about life on the airfield and telling us of the quiet life up there, the infrequent trips to Derry, and the shortage of work before the war. I lit my pipe with her laughing at the bowl's size. Margaret beckoned the child over, sat him on her knee and produced the toy and chocolate from her satchel.

The sound of footsteps outside interrupted his appraisal and, shooting from her knee, he streaked to the door as a shortish, thickset man in working clothes entered, squinting against the dark. 'It's two from the airfield, Bull,' his wife said, already egg-cracking at the fire. 'And his name's Bull, too.'

'Ah! From the airfield then?' He shook hands firmly with us both. 'Well now, I was working there when it was building. ''Twas a good time then, a fine time.' His eyes lit up as he spoke of the regular wages and the building materials he'd obtained on the cheap. I reflected then (as often since) that life for the workers without war or the threat of it tends to be of an inferior quality.

After a replica of our meal had disappeared with a final wipe of the plate we all sat round the fire, Bull kicking the soft turf with a thick-soled boot that would have been removed but for us, the child lying contentedly on his corduroy knees hugging the toy. Bull looked the least bit surprised as Margaret produced cigarettes and lit one herself. As we puffed and chatted, the child fell asleep and was removed gently by his mother. Margaret was leaning towards the fire, face blushed by the heat. The scene has remained with me, one of life's set pieces, which has attained the quality of a Rembrandt etching.

There were a few more visits, the last made while Margaret was on a short home leave. Before leaving for the mountain I raided the bedding store at the rear of the neighbouring unoccupied Nissen, and took with me sheets, pillowcases and blankets to add to rations horded or cadged. The booty, and especially the bedding, was received reverentially by Mrs Claffey. In the land of flax, new linen, readily obtainable off the ration, would have been a luxury not to be indulged until the old was threadbare. Bull was absent, but I left a quantity of tobacco and cigarettes.

I promised to write but knew I never would. After kissing the boy I turned to plant a chaste kiss on his mother's cheek, but was surprised by her grasping me in strong arms, offering her lips. The rush of pent-up desire nearly knocked me over and I clung on, pressing her head against my battledress blouse, as much to avoid her eyes as for support.

We broke as the child whimpered, perhaps sensing the final departure of his chocolate airman. There were tears in her eyes and in mine. 'Love to Bull,' I croaked. She nodded and I fled.

Vale Wellingtonia!

An entry in my log book of 7 June certified me as 'above average' as a General Reconnaissance pilot, one below 'exceptional'. Perhaps if I hadn't pranged the Oxford I might have made the ultimate grade! The squadron CO called me for an interview; said he was recommending me for a commission and took my agreement for granted. As a married man with a child, the extra pay would be acceptable, and a commission might help in the civvy street career market so, swallowing the unexpired portion of my socialist principles, I concurred.

Soon afterwards, the squadron received orders to fly *en masse* to the mainland. Our destination was Leicester East, an airfield within cycling distance of Betty's parental home, where she was living with the infant Susan. We gathered that the airfield was now occupied by a Transport Command conversion unit, though whether or not we were to be groomed for this unglamorous role was not clear – perhaps it was merely the most convenient repository for our Wimpys.

Margaret was one of the considerable gathering outside the control tower to see us leave. A squadron take-off was always a crowd-puller, though any hopes the watchers might have entertained about a fighter-type beat-up were disappointed. We would be two crews plus key groundstaff per aircraft, and anyway, Binevenagh frowned on frivolity.

She stood a little apart, very erect, as we rumbled down the runway. White blob of face under dead-straight cap . . . raised arm . . . fluttered hand . . . gone! Like so many more figures in the tapestry of the last four years, never to be seen again. When, years later, I saw the film version of Aidan Higgins' novel, *Langrishe Go Down*, about two sisters staying on in their crumbling County Kildare home, I immediately identified Margaret with Judi Dench, who played the principal character, Helen.

The loose gaggle of weathered white aircraft sweeping across middle England from the Irish Sea must have been an unusual sight for our celebrating countrymen as overland flights *en masse* by Coastal Command aircraft were rare. I shared Wellington G with Flight Lieutenant 'Sixty' Hill, so nicknamed because his father had been wounded in the battle for Hill Sixty on the Western Front. The aircraft was grossly overloaded with both people and plunder – Guinness being broached *en route* by all but the flight crew.

I persuaded Sixty to yield the controls as we approached Leicester on the grounds that I was familiar with the airfield's position and layout, which was untrue. I think he realised what I was up to when I circled the western suburbs in the hope of identifying *Greyfell*. I hadn't been able to let Nellie know about the day and time of the flight, but as the family had seen snaps of the Wimpy I thought that if anyone was at home they might put two and two together. Sixty, impatient and a little annoyed, exercised his seniority, took the controls and made a ropey landing to good-natured derision from the Guinness-happy passengers.

My pirouette over Braunstone had been unobserved – Nellie had anyway been on the round. By that stage of the war people were so *blasé* about aerial activity that it would have taken a repeat of the R101 airship's ghostly flight over the city in 1930 to bring them out on the avenues. But Betty spotted the aircraft lining up to land, as her mother's house was pretty well on the Leicester East circuit, and assumed that it was us.

I don't recall shedding any tears over abandoning the Wellingtons to their fate – which would almost certainly have been the knacker's yard, though some limped on in the RAF or foreign service for a few years. The only complete survivor, a Mark X Bomber Command version, is in the RAF Museum, Hendon, though a partially reconstructed Mark 1A resides at Brooklands near Weybridge, birthplace of some of the 11,400 Wimpys produced, where its remains were taken after recovery in September 1985 from Loch

Ness, where it had ditched in 1940 after an engine failure. It has now been substantially restored and is well worth a visit since its geodetic structure – looking oddly like the sperm whale's skeleton in my copy of *Moby Dick* – has been left partially exposed.

Had I put my 'war gratuity' towards the purchase of a redundant Mark XIV and preserved it in Uncle Harry's cavernous barn it would have given the cows something interesting to ruminate over – and been available to star in the epic film that never was: *Light Over Biscay*!

Wellington recovered from Loch Ness, on show at Brooklands, Weybridge

Breakthrough in Biscay and beyond

In the early summer of 1942, a Wellington of 172 Squadron, one of the first five to be fitted with the Leigh Light and now ready for action, illuminated and attacked an enemy submarine in the south-western area of the Bay, crippling though not sinking it. Post-war records identified it as an Italian vessel which survived a series of further misfortunes to end its operational career in the Japanese navy

– a bizarre end to the tragi-comedy of a nation of Puccinis propelled towards *Götterdämmerung* by its Wagnerian ally.

Altogether, during June and July 1942 there were eleven sightings and six Leigh Light attacks, with one sinking and two damaged – not a large number, but the consequences were dramatic and immediate. Unaware that there were only five aircraft fitted with what his shaken U-boaters were calling *'das verdammte Licht'*, Admiral Doenitz lost his nerve and ordered crews to reverse the normal procedure of crossing the Bay submerged during the day, and surfacing to recharge their batteries at night.

This change of tactics produced something of a bonanza for the daylight air patrols over the Bay, with many more sightings and some kills, though part of the gilt was removed from the gingerbread when U-boat armament was improved, causing some losses among attacking aircraft, which increased when hunting packs of JU 88 fighters were drafted in, inevitably leading to a free-for-all once Beaufighters and Mosquitos based in Cornwall joined in.

With the fitting, towards the end of 1942, of a somewhat Heath Robinson, though effective, device to U-boats which enabled them to detect radar transmissions from patrolling aircraft up to thirty miles distant, they were ordered to resume the former practice of 'dive by day, surface for battery-charging by night', and the number of sightings fell dramatically.

The introduction by the Allies, early in 1943, of centimetric radar – which the German device couldn't detect – reversed the trend, and there was a further surge in the number of sightings and attacks, with two kills being credited to 172 Squadron.

The Germans never did get on top of the new radar, though Air Chief Marshal Harris's insistence, backed by Churchill, that a version be fitted to his strategic bomber force meant that the secret would be out once an aircraft equipped with it had fallen into enemy hands – as Coastal Command's top brass had pointed out.

This happened quite quickly when a Stirling bomber was shot down over Holland, though for some reason – possibly because they were concentrating on rocketry – the Reich boffins failed in their quest to provide the U-boat fleet with a means of detecting the new radar signals.

This gave 19 Group of Coastal Command the chance they had long been waiting for. All U-boats proceeding to or from their heavily fortified bases on the French coast passed through the Bay, normally under cover of darkness. Now, with a reasonably adequate fleet of aircraft, including four-engine types, it was possible to mount more intensive patrols, which soon led to a useful increase in the number of sightings and night attacks.

Although the number of confirmed kills remained small, Doenitz again ordered his U-boats to submerge by night and surface in daylight, though, as before, this soon petered out and it was back to 'up night, down day'.

It was in mid-Atlantic in the early summer of 1943 that the decisive battle was joined. The year had started badly for the allied convoys, with particularly heavy losses in February and March threatening to torpedo the Alliance's whole convoy strategy. But by now an increasing number of long-range aircraft were becoming available – many with Leigh Lights, centimetric radar and a new weapon, homing aerial torpedoes. The deployment of shorter-range aircraft such as Swordfish, operating from escort carriers, was also proving effective.

By May, U-boat losses had become unsustainable and Doenitz recalled his entire North Atlantic fleet, enabling Allied convoys to pass through the dreaded mid-Atlantic gap without loss. U-boats continued to operate in the Central Atlantic area, but American escort carriers did such slaughter in the waters round the Azores that Doenitz also withdrew his forces from this area. The Battle of the Atlantic had been won.

A graphic and moving account of this final phase in the long-running battle – and indeed of the whole U-boat campaign – seen through the eyes of Herbert A Werner, one of Doenitz's most successful commanders, is given in his book *Iron Coffins*, first published in this country in 1970.*

---

* Published in paperback by Pan Books in 1972

COOK'S TOUR

Flying a Rolls

1333 Transport Conversion Unit operated the Douglas DC3, the militarised US airliner widely used for transporting troops and equipment, with a starring role at the Battle of Arnhem (in which the comedian Jimmy Edwards won his DFC). Its nickname, 'Dakota', rang a bell since a fellow pupil at Moosejaw had strayed over the US border on a night exercise in his Harvard, run short of fuel and, after circling for some time, managed to land in a field guided by the car headlights of quick-witted North Dakotans who, though they were unable to refuel the aircraft, had no difficulty fuelling the pilot.

My commission came through quite quickly and I was soon being measured for the new uniform by Messrs Routen & Mitchell, a pair of cheerful tailors who ran their tapes over Nellie's bespoke customers. Permission was obtained to live out and I cycled to and fro throughout the two-month posting, passing the golf course in whose bunkers Betty and I had spent many romantic moments during my leaves.

Spending little time on the station, I lost touch with the 172 crew, who were soon posted elsewhere, though I later cycled over to the airfield in Lincolnshire where second dicky Harry was converting to Stirlings (which he confirmed as flying coffins). Later, Paddy got in touch and stayed with us for a couple of days, captivating my mother-in-law with his blarney.

Myself and a number of other 172 pilots learned that we now faced a concentrated course of day and night flying which would include paratroop and container drops, glider towing, cross-country and formation flying, all to ready us for a Far East posting where it was expected that the Japanese would fight to the end in a Nipponese version of *Götterdämmerung*.

The course started in mid-July and they kept us busy. One morning in August, breakfast was accompanied by the news that something called an atom bomb had been dropped by the Americans on

Hiroshima. Not being scientifically brilliant at school I was unaware of the significance of splitting the atom, having always thought it small enough, but was impressed when, after a second bomb was dropped on Nagasaki, the Japanese surrendered.

The course continued, and any hope of an early return to civvy street was quashed when it was made known that we were still to be sent overseas to relieve aircrew who had been out there for years in what had become known as the *Forgotten War*. Although this was a bit of a blow it did seem as if what might have been a Dicey Do would now be in the nature of a Cook's Tour at His Majesty's expense.

The urging of the little orderly-room corporal at Harrogate to put by a proportion of my pay had fallen on far from fertile ground, but with family responsibilities I resolved to emulate Scrooge from now on (and anyway, it seemed unlikely that there would be much to spend money on overseas). So it turned out, and in addition to new-found frugality I was able to employ my Nellie genes in modest enterprises.

Wing-waggling over the pram in the garden (wondering whether the rasping engines would disturb sleeping Susan) was an early diversion until mother-in-law's neighbours got up a petition complaining about low flying aircraft. The Pratt & Whitneys *were* on the noisy side – as were the Harvard's Wasp, especially on changing from coarse to fine pitch. The Americans seemed to have nothing as silky smooth as the Merlin which powered the Spitfire and Hurricane, and even the Wimpy's Hercules had a soothing whistle. We put it down to the aerial equivalent of their noisy entrance to a bar, mopping up the talent!

All went smoothly in the air, except on an occasion when I was airborne with one of the ex-172 pilots during a night glider-towing exercise. Just as the aircraft took off with him at the controls, we experienced a loss of power and saw the boundary hedge looming ahead. The throttles had slipped back! I jammed them forward and, with a roar, we just cleared the hedge. Afterwards, the glider pilot said he had been about to cast off the tow hawser, certain that we were doomed.

A trifling error occurred on a paratrooping exercise to Ringway airport near Manchester when I landed at the civil, instead of the military, airfield, but after jokes all round we took off and landed next door. In retrospect, I think that some of us might have been suffering from operational fatigue. I certainly couldn't blame the aircraft – flying the DC3 was like driving a Rolls Royce after lurching along in a tank. There was even a proper seat for the co-pilot, far more comfortable than the rarely used fold-down contrivance in the Wimpy.

At the end of August I passed as a 'proficient' transport pilot and, the course having ended, awaited the overseas posting. It was mid-October before the call came so I had a pleasant five or six weeks of visiting. Nellie, my sisters and the maiden aunts seemed pleased that earlier fulminations against the marital state had come to nothing. I became a proficient pram-pusher, though a *Greyfell* neighbour shot me a scornful look when I explained that I was wheeling my daughter along the avenue while her mother was at a rugby match with Peggy's husband.

On 16 October a clutch of us took off as passengers in an Avro York, a half-hearted transport conversion of the Lancaster, for a three-day flight to Karachi (then in India) via Malta, Cairo and Shaibah – a god-forsaken desert staging-post which had inspired the unfortunates marooned there to compose the dirge-like *Shaibah Blues*.

During a ten-day stay in a tented camp near Karachi, frazzled by the heat, I had the first unnerving experience of using an Indian loo-hole with a beady-eyed 'untouchable' squatting at the bottom, as impatient as the Misses Winks to dispose of the solids. A stately bearded and turbaned man dropped by to measure us for shorts, shirts and bush jackets, which were delivered the next day, putting Nellie's merry tailors to shame. Then it was on across India to Calcutta in a Sunderland flying boat, wondering whether one ought to salute the quarterdeck on boarding. The friendly squadron leader skipper, noting the ribbon of the recently awarded Atlantic Star campaign medal, let me try the controls for several spells during the flight, though he took over well before we touched down on the Hoogli river.

After a couple of days seeing the sights it was on to Rangoon in a DC3 – where I met Betty's elder brother Gordon, now a major, who was encamped awaiting repatriation after long and distinguished service in Burma, which had earned him a mention in despatches. He handed me his Sten sub-machine gun to defend myself against the dacoits – bandits – who he said were active in those parts. I never came across any, although, on a visit to Hong Kong races, I was told that a jockey in one of the events had been shot on the way round by dacoits or their local equivalents because by leading the field he was upsetting the odds.

Mingaladon

Our destination was some miles north of Rangoon, with a name suggesting more a tinkling of temple bells than an airfield. Mingaladon occupied an area of jungly scrub established to provide a base for various units during the long and bitter Burma campaign, including a brief stay by Chenault's Flying Tigers during the Japanese bombing of Rangoon and, later, a Spitfire squadron whose brand new replacement aircraft, still crated, were recently said to have been buried somewhere on the site following the Japanese surrender, though efforts to find them have so far been unsuccessful.

The airfield was now home to 267 Squadron of Transport Command, its Dakotas bearing the flying horse badge symbolising the squadron's role in transporting troops and supplies throughout the long Burmese campaign.

Accommodation was mainly in tents, and the runways were of steel mesh. There was a large building which housed a theatre in which, we were told, a recent showing of the film *Henry V* starring Laurence Olivier had been greeted with boos and shouts of: 'We want Betty Grable!' *The* pinup girl of the time, look-alike Grables adorned the fuselages of Flying Fortresses and Liberators as well as the living quarters of a million GIs. It was common knowledge that when Jackie

Cooper, her former husband, was posted to the Pacific theatre, fellow GIs would walk miles to hear at first hand what she was like in bed.

I was based at Mingaladon for five months until repatriated at the end of April 1946, and have memories of magic carpet flights which the intervening years have done little to dim. Bangkok, Saigon, Butterworth, Kuala Lumpur. Palembang, Batavia, Soerabaya, Calcutta, Delhi and – jewel in the crown – Hong Kong, then magically returning to life after the years of occupation – evidenced by burnt-out residences of rich merchants on the Peak, and stories of unspeakable cruelty towards the poorer Chinese.

Mingaladon in the monsoon

The days of filling in the time between flights with frenetic activity were now past, and as soon as I was settled in my tent with co-pilot Johnnie, and 'George', a pleasant Burmese, to look after us, I was able to make several trips to Rangoon. There, I was ravished by the golden-domed Shwe Dagon pagoda and a proliferation of Buddhas and Goddesses – including a huge reclining version whose blissful expression and voluptuous pose would not have been out of place as nose-art on a Superfortress bomber.

Mingaladon in the sun

Travel was made easier after I had taken up brother-in-law Gordon's suggestion that I make myself known to the fellow officers of his final regiment (which occupied a site on a straight length of the road to Rangoon near the village of Insein, wittily but misleadingly nicknamed 'Round the Bend'). After surviving the hottest curry their mess could provide – the standard test for visitors – I was virtually adopted by the regiment, the Colonel volunteering the use of a Jeep and Indian driver whenever required.

I soon found that his generous gesture had been inspired by a measure of self-interest. With the prospect of early repatriation, he was bent on returning to wife and home bearing gifts, and learning that I expected soon to be departing for Hong Kong he wondered if I might make a few purchases for him. Of course I agreed, and after my next trip returned to the airfield with the goods, mainly silk lengths suitable for lingerie – which he received with trembling satisfaction. As he was in his forties with a waistline to match, I couldn't imagine him in the act of love, but hoped that neither he nor she would be disappointed as he was a friendly man and the jeep was a godsend.

The commercial possibilities of this constant transit between countries long cut-off from normal trading soon became apparent. There was a chronic shortage of cigarettes, and a tin of 'issue' Players could be bartered for a pair of hand-made shoes or exquisite items of Siamese silver in the market outside Bangkok airport.

More lucrative merchandise was revealed when John, a senior 267 pilot, crashed on landing at Saigon airport *en route* from Hong Kong to Mingaladon. There were only slight injuries, but among the scattered cargo were boxes of watches and jewellery he'd bought cheaply in Kowloon to sell to a contact in Rangoon for great profit. Though more honoured in the breach than the observance, there were rules which prohibited trading by service personnel, so John had to deny all knowledge of the contents as the service police impounded the horde.

He was grounded after the accident and his repatriation order came through shortly afterwards, frustrating the planned run to collect a last consignment. We occupied adjoining tents and swapped books, so when he asked if I would collect the goods and deliver them to his contact in Rangoon I agreed, and promised to remit the sale proceeds when repatriated – which I did. Never having expected to hear more, he insisted on splitting the proceeds, my share funding, among other things, a second-hand dinner service – most of which survives.

Rangoon idling

The Rangoon contact, a pleasant Indian shopkeeper in long shorts and black knee-length socks, pressed me to carry on the arrangement, which I agreed to do, though only on a more modest scale, dealing mainly in expanding metal watchstraps. I don't think Nellie would have disapproved of this lack of too-aggressive enterprise. The margin of profit was still indecently large compared with her own modest 33%, she having always been concerned more for her customers' friendship than in squeezing the last penny from the business.

Far more enjoyable than making money was judiciously spending it in the teeming markets and bazaars of the cities on our routes: exquisite Chinese puppets and ceramics from the Mahjong-clacking street markets of Hong Kong; a large ginger jar from Batavia purchased against a background of insurgent gunfire; and an egg-shaped silver ink pot whose supporting stags heads should have told me that it was made in Scotland! Most desirable of all were the carpets and rugs I acquired from a vast emporium in Calcutta presided over by one Abdul Kalik, a smoothly handsome Parsee.

That they were of high quality seemed to be confirmed when, many years later, Abdul turned up at our house in Leicester bent on buying them back. I was out at the time and a Canadian friend who was staying with us opened the door to him. 'Oh! Mr Harrison, I would have known you anywhere,' he cried, getting down on his knees to examine the Persian carpet in the sitting room. I was amazed that he'd survived the riots which broke out on partition as his high-handed treatment of those who worked for him, with his cry, 'Barbarians, sir, barbarians!' should have earned him a knife between the shoulder blades. He left carpetless before my return and I never heard from him again.

Rangoon pagoda

The Mingaladon log book entries nearly all have 'crew and passengers' as the payloads, but except for a few I don't recollect who the passengers were or why they were being shuttled between these exotic places.

Hong Kong, the author at The Peak

On one of the half-dozen trips to Hong Kong there was a contingent of friendly UK Fire Service officers who had volunteered to help reorganise the HK brigade. On another was a posse of senior police officers who we assumed were being parachuted in to apply the Kingdom's corruption-free principles to the Hong Kong force, so that it was a shock when they made it clear during the flight that they had no intention of relying on police pay, but would be open to offers 'on the side'. Making a bob or two in modest trading was one thing, undermining our faith in the incorruptibility of the British bobby another, so I made sure that the landing at Kaitak (then HK's airport, squeezed up against high ground) involved a turn onto the runway so steep that it put the wind up the crew, let alone the passengers!

The crew and I enjoyed complimentary front-row seats, and Nancy Nevinson, who had a small part in both plays, was pleasant company on shopping and sightseeing expeditions. She and I braved a Chinese opera, a performance of great length, alleviated by the performance of one Ma Tsu Tong, billed as the most famous comic in South China. Some years later, having asked a visiting delegation of Chinese government officials whether they had ever come across *Mao Tse Dung*, the famous comedian, the interpreter returned a blank stare.

Shakespeare programme

During a chat with Gielgud on the first leg of the flight to Bangkok he had asked if our route would take us anywhere near the ruins of Angkor Wat, the ancient temple complex in Cambodia, and if so, whether it might be possible to fly over the site (which he'd read about in Osbert Sitwell's travel book, *Escape With Me.**) I said I'd read the paperback and on an overnight stop in Saigon had asked recently-returned French colonials whether there was any possibility of an overland visit. *Pas possible* had been the answer, accompanied by shrugged shoulders and raised eyebrows.

John Gielgud, pictured seven years later in 1953

Doug, the navigator, found that it was almost on the track of our next leg, Bangkok to Saigon, though his charts indicated a lot of jungle

---

* *First published 1939 by Macmillan*

and he'd run into tricky weather conditions on previous trips. There was some excitement in the rear as we neared the destination, but though I circled the estimated position at a height of two hundred feet there was nothing to be seen but an unbroken carpet of green, so we both had to be satisfied with Osbert's descriptive powers, but could at least boast of having hovered over the sacred spot.

Angkor Wat, now reclaimed from the jungle

Passing down the passenger compartment later to inform them of our approach to Hong Kong, and finding an animated conversation in progress, I heard for the first and last time the theatrical equivalent of 'Stop talking shop!' and its RAF version, 'Close the hangar doors!' '*Everyone knows the curtains close!*' rang out in Gielgud's exquisitely moderated tones, words I have since employed to head off dinner party boasts of increased property values.

My last flight, on 27 April 1946, was from Dum Dum airport, Delhi, to Mingaladon, in what I remember as Monsoon weather. I was profoundly relieved when we bounced down on the metal landing strip and, cutting the engines for the last time, I decided that return to a *terra firma* existence (the more *firma* the less terror!) would suit me well, having flown a total of 1400 hours since that first flight in a Tiger Moth.

The return home was by sea, slow but reasonably comfortable. Disembarking at Liverpool, I travelled by train to a demob centre near Leeds where, walking in a recently-promoted F/O, I emerged a plain Mister, with a parting gift from His Majesty – reach-me-down sports coat and flannels – which Nellie excoriated almost as strongly as she had the wide-shouldered sports coat I'd brought back from Canada!

ALF REVISITED

In 1968 I moved with my family to Nottingham after years of peregrination in the cause of career enhancement. Nellie had been living with us for five years, having been whisked away to the north of England, where I had started a new job, after her acrimonious parting from Peggy and her husband (with whom she'd been living in a specially designed wing of their new house).

Nellie had been quite fond of Dolly, the younger of my two aunts, as had I, and with her health deteriorating it seemed apt and timely, now that we were back in the Midlands, to attempt a burial of the hatchet wielded in the final bust-up with Grandpa, which had of course numbered Dolly and Orpha among the incidental casualties. I made the approach (which was warmly welcomed) and both Dolly and Jim, with Orpha and her second husband, attended our eldest daughter Susan's wedding.

After Nellie's death in 1969, I managed with great difficulty to trace Alf after finding that his Great War disability pension was still being paid, and much to his surprise came face-to-face with him – in Margate of all places. That dramatic (but not unpleasant) confrontation had its amusing side, and I'll never forget the moment after the flat door opened to my knock and I posed the question, 'I don't suppose you know who I am?' – or his reply: 'You must be Graham.'

We chatted for a while in the poky little flat, and I learned that the rather sad-looking woman in the mantelpiece photograph had died not long ago, leaving him on his own. We strolled down to the pier where I stood him lunch, and still recall the half-amused glances exchanged as we downed our pints. Later, I took him to my hotel for tea and showed him the family photographs I'd brought, which I suppose was a bit thoughtless as Nellie was young-looking until well into middle age, Peggy and Mildred had acquired well-set-up husbands, and my RAF snapshots gave the impression of an action-packed war. When I told him of my post-war qualification as a solicitor he must ruefully have realised that we hadn't suffered unduly from his absence. After the visit there was some desultory correspondence, but it became clear that he didn't want to maintain contact and it lapsed. I never saw or heard from him again.

I suppose I might have been more confrontational about his desertion when we met, but his circumstances seemed so poor that I hadn't the heart. The feeling I had (and still have) is that it was probably for the best – we'd been better off without him. Neither Mildred nor I had missed him as badly as had Peg, then in early adolescence. She had been very fond of him, and he of her, and I think she always felt that Nellie's temper and lack of tolerance had much to do with his defection. Before her death Peg told Mildred that on the day of his final disappearance she'd waited, as usual, for him to meet her at the school gate and walk home with her. For days afterwards she lingered there at going-home time 'knowing' that he would turn up as he had in the past, but of course he never did. The expected letter from him never came.

In the mid-seventies, after we had moved to the West Country, Dolly telephoned with amazing news. She had heard from a John Harrison who had come across her address in a letter from someone called Graham, found among his recently deceased father's papers. Did she know who this might be?

This John lived in Broadstairs and was, of course, Alf's son, my stepbrother. I made contact, found that he was married with two daughters, and invited them to stay with us for the weekend. At Bath station I recognised him immediately – a truer version of Alf than I, a typical Bennett. We got on well, and could hardly stop talking as we turned the pages of photograph albums. My late wife and I visited them, and in 1992 John and I went on a tour of the Great War battlefields, something that he'd wanted to do with Alf for years but could never persuade him.

He was not well during the tour and, after a painful illness, died in 1995. Later, I wrote the following account as a celebration of our brief relationship, and a sort of laying of Alf's ghost.

HIGH WOOD

September 1992 . . . The coach ran smoothly through the Picardy countryside, passing the many military cemeteries which for almost eighty years had been laying the balm of their ordered tranquillity on the century's first great wound.

The tall ex-major leading the battlefields tour had concluded his outline of the Somme offensive, and songs from *Oh! What a Lovely War* were doing their bit towards capturing the spirit of the times:

> *No more church parades on Sunday,*
> *No more putting in for leave,*
> *I shall kiss the Sergeant-Major,*
> *How I'll miss him, how he'll grieve . . .*

I glanced sideways at my half-brother. Amazing, the likeness – even to the peak of hair clinging sparsely to the forward position, covering the retreat of the flanks. But no dent on the left temple where shiny skin had healed over the shrapnel wound.

That fascinating concavity was the sharpest image I'd retained of my father – our father. There weren't many others. I'd just turned eight when the slightly abstracted man finally decamped after several trial runs. Just over sixty years ago. A bit of a mother's boy, it had all rather washed over me, though my elder sister had taken it badly.

'We're now approaching one of the larger cemeteries.' The major's voice cut in on the music. 'Most of those lying here fell on the first of July, opening day of the Somme offensive. We haven't time to stop but I've asked the driver to slow down.' 'Lying here' . . . 'fell' . . . The anodyne words were kindly meant to soften the image of young men slowly walking through the summer storm of steel.

The major leant over us, a kindly stork, as the ranks of dazzling white gravestones slow-marched past the windows. 'High Wood's coming up soon. I'll give an outline of the battle, then perhaps one of you could come up with the personal angle.'

I nodded towards my half-brother. 'John'll do it. I knew very little of dad's exploits until he turned up.' It was true – there'd been a few sepia snapshots of a kilted man carrying a swagger stick, and a half-remembered story about cadging a spoonful of jam from the occupants of a neighbouring shell-hole, who'd later been blown up, ending with his sergeant's grumble: 'Pity you didn't bring the whole jar.'

Wry humour, though snapshots in the album John had brought along soon after we'd discovered each other showed a man growing sadder by the year, as if his buried past were surfacing. 'He was cagey about the post-war years,' John had recalled. 'I always suspected he had something to hide.'

By God he had! A wife and three kids abandoned and no word from him ever again. And what about his second 'marriage'? Ma had never sought a divorce – or re-married: 'Once is enough!'

British troops, some in kilts, near High Wood, October 1916

'Delville Wood and High Wood.' The major was on his feet again. 'Both on high ground . . . vital they should be taken . . . fiercely defended . . . hand-to-hand fighting . . . heavy casualties on both sides.'

My mind disengaged itself as the creeping barrage of phrases rolled over me. The open fields, shorn of their crops, looked peaceful under the September sun, though spaced-out men in berets walking with shotguns at the port were an odd reminder of the distant clash of armies. Start of the hunting season – no armistice for birds and rabbits!

John had now taken the microphone. 'I didn't know I had a brother till dad died. There were letters among his papers. I followed the trail and found Graham at the end of it.' I took up the narrative. 'I did manage to trace dad through his disablement pension after mother died in '69. I got in touch, we had a friendly meeting, but it soon became obvious that he didn't want to maintain a relationship and my letters went unanswered. But at least he knew that there were no hard feelings.'

John frowned. 'I find it difficult to forgive him for not letting on to Graham about me. I was an only one – we'd have had extra years together. But water under the bridge – and anyway here we are. I always wanted dad to take me back to the battlefields, but he never did. Now we're doing it for him!'

The coach was slowing down as he continued. 'He joined up soon after the outbreak of war, and by some means got into a Scottish regiment – the Cameronians. He took part in several battles, but it was here at High Wood that he got his *Blighty*.'

As if on cue, the coach turned right into a dirt road which led steeply upwards towards a dense crown of trees. 'Dad was in the thick of the battle for the wood.' The tone was more solemn now. 'The platoon officer, sergeant and a lot of his pals were killed or wounded, and though only a lance corporal he led the remainder in a bayonet charge. That was where he got his wounds – a serious one in the head and another in the thigh.'

The coach came to rest in the dark shadow of the wood. I shivered, oppressed by the brooding silence as John continued. 'He lay there all day before the stretcher-bearers were able to get him to the field dressing station. The surgeon who operated later said it was a miracle he was still alive.'

We all sat in silence until the major's voice broke the spell. 'Half an hour to look round, but the wood's out of bounds. All sorts of battle debris still in there. It's a sort of graveyard.'

Memorial to the Cameron Highlanders, High Wood

All grouped beside a stark granite memorial commemorating the Scots who had died in the battle. Then John and I took up positions on either side of it as the cameras clicked in the otherwise respectful silence. The rest trooped off along the fenced perimeter, leaving the two of us standing there. I closed my eyes, trying to visualize the scene at the height of the assault – shell bursts churning up the sodden clay, machine guns scything the undergrowth, khaki and grey bodies hugging the earth, many in a last embrace.

John broke the silence. 'He always seemed old to me, but it's suddenly hit me – he was only in his twenties when he lay there.' His voice was strained, and glancing at him I saw the lips tightly compressed in a white face. Tears stung my eyes as I put an arm round his shoulder, seeking words of comfort.

'Well at least he had some happy years with you – was a good father . . . I mean he stuck it out – stayed with you . . .' Even as I spoke I saw the irony of elevating this minimal requirement into a high standard of fatherhood.

'Yes, he stayed, and was good in his way to mother and me. But I never felt he was really with us – in spirit I mean.' He frowned. 'Half the time his mind seemed to be elsewhere.' He turned to me with a wry smile. 'Maybe with you, his other family.'

I shook my head. 'No, not with us.' I nodded towards the darkly silent wood. 'In there with his dead pals. Now I've seen it I wouldn't think he had much left to give anyone when he came out of there.'

The major was now counting his returning sheep onto the coach, watched by a group of munching hunters, their guns piled peacefully in tripods as if awaiting the curling tendrils of runner beans. The sunlight was weaker now, but in contrast to the wood's brooding shade seemed summery.

As we settled into our seats I experienced a feeling of deep satisfaction at our having made the visit together, but more than that felt that I'd been granted understanding. As in a grainy silent film, scenes from childhood were re-run from the viewpoint of the young man who had lain wounded in the wood. There was the terraced house, fit perhaps for an untroubled hero, but prison for one whose nights drew him back to the darkened wood. There mother Nellie, clear-visioned and ambitious, convinced that if he would only turn teetotal all would be well, whereas everyone but she was aware that he totally abhorred tea! And always, inside, an emptiness until he had done what in battle he had never done – cut and run.

'Wish I'd made more effort to keep in touch.' I looked sadly at the retreating hilltop. 'Though I suppose you can't reshape the past.'

'No, but at least we found each other.' John patted my knee, grinning. 'And I always wanted a brother. Even an old guy like you's better than nothing!'

I returned an affectionate punch. Yes, if Alf's troubled spirit was still haunting the wood, perhaps the sight of us standing there had given it quietus. 'I'm glad we came.'

John grinned. 'Me too. I think we've laid the old lad's ghost.'

AFTERWORD

The Harrison Family

Graham's RAF service ended in the Spring of 1946 after a five-month swansong in the Far East flying an American DC3 Dakota – luxurious after rattling round in the wartime Wimpy. It was then back to civvy street and the responsibilities of a married man where, after resuming his local government career, Graham qualified as a solicitor, eventually becoming secretary and solicitor to the Wessex Water Authority.

Having always had ambitions as a writer, Graham began to bombard legal and professional journals with articles of a humorous flavour under the pen-name *H. Grayson*, even achieving brief glory in the late-lamented *Punch*. Eventually he became for almost twenty years the weekly writer of the satirical 'endpiece' in the *Local Government Review*. The *Review*'s editor published a collection of his pieces and persuaded him to write a novel, titled *The Last Alderman*.

Graham's first wife Betty with children Sarah, Robert, Susan, David & Jane

After the death of Graham's first wife Betty, mother of their five children, Graham re-married. He and Sue live near Bath and have two children.

Graham & Sue with their children Bryony and Tom – RAF Club, Piccadilly

The 70th Anniversary of the Battle of the Atlantic

The seventieth anniversary of the victory was celebrated in May 2013 with a service in Liverpool Cathedral, and functions organised by the Royal Navy and the Coastal Command and Maritime Air Association in Liverpool, Pembroke Dock (South Wales) and Cornwall.

At a dinner in Newquay as part of the Cornish celebration, I found myself the only one of the hundred or so present who had taken part in the Battle, and I suppose there couldn't have been all that many survivors at the other events.

Son Tom and daughter Bryony who accompanied me were duly impressed, though I was brought to earth the following day during a visit to the restored Shackleton reconnaissance aircraft at St Mawgan airfield in Cornwall. After viewing the bewildering array of dials and levers in the cockpit, Tom expressed the thought that was running through my own head:

'Pa, I can't imagine you coping with anything like this. Now you have to ask us to change channels on the television!'

Made in the USA
Columbia, SC
29 April 2017